Business Management Philosophy

Written by:

Mr. Louis Rubin

List of Advisories

Advisory 1

Business Entrepreneurism

1. *Definition of business.*   In everyday speech, the word "business" does not possess a clear-cut meaning.   It is applied rather vaguely to trading and manufacturing occupations as distinguished from the arts and professions.

For the purpose of our study, business may be defined as follows:

Any occupation in which men, at the risk of loss, seek to make money by producing commodities, or by hiring the services of others for utilization at a profit.

Or, more briefly:

Business is any gainful occupation of which profit is the goal and in which there is a risk of loss.

This definition, like most others, fits some cases rather loosely.   The farmer, for example, can be said to be in business only in so far as he hires labor and markets his products.   As he enlarges his operations and hires more men to work for him, he becomes more and more a business man because he is more and more concerned with the typically business problems involved in accounting, management, salesmanship and credits.

More evidently, the rural storekeeper is in business, for he buys goods in the hope of selling them at a profit and takes the risk of not being able to do so. The clerk in his employ on a salary takes no business risk and is not thinking about profits; hence strictly speaking, he is not a business man. But he is part of a business machine and is learning how to do business, and so is commonly thought of as being in business.

The owner of a factory who buys raw materials and hires labor is taking risks and is in business. Some of his employees are workers with tolls and machines; they are not directly concerned with business problems, and are not thought of as being in business. Other employees, such as those connected with the purchasing or the sales department, may have to assume distinctly business responsibilities; we think of them as being in business.

The bookkeeper who keeps the records of purchases, sales, output, costs, etc., stands on the border line between business and manual labor. As a mere bookkeeper, he is little more than a machine, but as a potential accountant, able to improve his employer's system of bookkeeping and to warn him against the danger of increasing costs, he steps into the ranks of business men.

In general, the great mass of laborers in manufacturing establishments and on our railroads, whose work is mainly with their hands, are not thought of as business men although they are connected with business enterprises. They have no part in the solution of problems involving risk and profit, and are not being trained for such efforts. They have "jobs" in business concerns, but they assume no business responsibilities. On the other hand, every business enterprise employs men upon whom the employer unloads some of his responsibilities. Such men, from cashiers to department managers, are in direct contact with business problems and are regarded as business men even though their own money might not be at risk.

2. *Profit and Risk are essential elements*. It I s not important to decide whether this or that man is in business, but it is important to understand that the word "business" necessarily implies a financial statement upon which two most

important words are profit and loss. If profit is not the goal, then the enterprise is not a business one.

By the profit of a business enterprise is meant the income left over after all the costs and expenses have been paid. A small storekeeper doing a cash business must sell his goods at such prices and in such volume as will enable him to pay the wages of his employees, a fair wage to himself, rent to his landlord, interest on capital invested, and all other expenses. If, at the end of the year, his inventory shows that his stock of goods has not shrunk in value and his outstanding debts are no greater, the increase or decrease of his bank balance during the year will disclose his profit or loss.

Profit is the goal of business. In later chapters, we shall make a closer study of profit and endeavor to show how profits are earned, and against what odds. We shall also see that the struggle for profits which we call business has been a tremendous force in the development of human capacity and in the advancement of civilization.

3. *Importance of money and price*. At the present time almost all goods are made to be sold. Specialization and the subdivision of labor have been carried so far that few men produce the things which they themselves consume. Old people recall the days when farmers had little need for cash, for they bought little at the stores. Their own farms produced most of their food and material for some of their clothing. Today the average farmer in the United States and Canada devotes his energies to the raising of a few crops. He sells these for money and buys much of his food and all his cloths.

So it happens that money and prices have become very important matters. What men really want are goods and commodities, things which possess what we call value. To get these is the ultimate object of work, but under modern conditions the immediate reward of work is money-with money the things wanted can be purchased. By the price of a thing is meant the amount of money it sells for. Evidently the subject of money and its purchasing power is of great importance to all people.

Since business men must figure their profits in money and cannot make a profit unless they sell at a price higher than they bought, it is evident that the forces which control the purchasing power of money must not be ignored by the wide-awake business man. Thar is why the subject of money and prices and credit are so fully treated in modern business texts.

4. *Business must satisfy human wants*. Although the business man is seeking to make a profit for himself, he must nevertheless think more of others than of himself. He can earn profit only through his ability to please others. If he is a trader, he must buy and sell things that people want. He is not a dictator and cannot make people buy his goods merely because he himself thinks they are better than the goods people call for. So the business man must study human wants and caprices. He may not approve of their tastes or of their judgement, but if he wishes to make a profit, he must be ruled by them. He may be a manufacturer of shoes and know very well that high heels make walking painful, but he will not let what he knows about physiology and anatomy shape the model of any woman's shoe- unless possibly his wife's.

P.D. Armour once said that he chose to deal with pork because it was an article of food that nearly everybody wanted in some form or another. A business dealing in a commodity that is in universal demand, such as wheat, flour, or cotton cloth. Is capable of tremendous development. The profit on each barrel of flour or each gallon of oil may be small, yet the gross profits may run into the millions because of the large sales.

5. *New wants are constantly appearing*. A remarkable development of machine production characterizes our century. Invention after invention has lowered the costs of production and made possible a great increase in the output of commodities. One man with the aid of modern machinery is able to produce many times what his grandfather could produce fifty or sixty years ago, or his father thirty years ago.

Nevertheless, the efficiency of the machine has not pleased everybody. Some pessimistic souls have seen in its tireless output only the bogey of overproduction, with goods of every description piled high in the manufacturers' warehouses for want of buyers. Such pessimism is based upon a fallacy, namely, the assumption that a man has a definite number of wants and that when these are satisfied he will be content.

As a matter of fact, man is a bundle of an infinite number of potential wants. This is one of the important characteristics which distinguish man from all other animals. A certain amount of food and drink, a little play-a chance to run and climb a

6

tree or now and then to "lay" for a mouse or chipmunk-will bring complete content to the most high-bred tabby in any cat show. The wants of all the lower animals are fixed in number, and when these are gratified, the animal is ready for sleep.

But man is insatiable. As his power over nature grows of his wealth increases, his wants multiply. When poor and half-nourished, his idea of heaven is a roast beef and vegetables. A poor and ignorant Yankee farmer was once asked what he was working for. "Salt pork and sundown," was his illuminating reply. He wanted the day to end so that he might get something to eat and go to bed. If that farmer should inherit a fortune and go to New York City to live, it needs no prophet to foretell what would happen to his taste for salt pork, or that sundown might become a signal for more exciting than going to bed.

6. *The overproduction bogey*. Fortunately for the business producer, as well as for the man who wishes to sell his services, there is not the slightest possibility that the world will ever be overstocked with the things that men desire. General overproduction has no significance in the business except when it is applied to a single commodity. The introduction of the automobile brought about a temporary overproduction of horses, wagons, and harnesses. The increasing use of gas and electricity led to a glut in the kerosene lamp market. Some people prefer rice to potatoes, both having substantially the same value as food; if this taste for rice should spread rapidly throughout the country, then there might be an overproduction of potatoes.

Since the business man is striving to make a profit, he must constantly be on his guard, whether he be manufacturer or trader, against overproduction or overstocking in special lines, and seek to anticipate the changes of demand to which the market is susceptible. He need have no fear that any increase in the production of goods will so satiate the human race that there will be no desire for his services. As production increases, wealth will increase, and the demand for goods will not only be greater but will also be more varied.

7. *Importance of salesmanship and advertising*. The reader has gathered from the two preceding sections not only how necessary it is for the business nab to study the wants of his customers, but also how important it is that he be able to give them just what they want. To sell a man anything, you must first know what he wants and then be able to convince him that

you can supply it at a reasonable price. In the old days of so-called community production and marketing, when there were no railways or steamships, both production and trading were usually on a small scale and the business man knew most of his customers personally. Now, however, production and marketing are world affairs. A manufacturer in a Massachusetts village may sell in all the continents of the globe. Thus it happens that marketing has become one of the most important of business problems. No one can succeed in business if he ignores its difficulties and its perils.

Advertising and salesmanship, which are vital parts of the marketing process, have special importance in any business which deals with something new. The salesman and the advertisement must rouse in people a desire for that new thing. The manufacturer cannot afford to wait for the slow development of his industry that will ensue if he lets the advantages of his product be discovered gradually as a result of its use among a small amount of customers. Hence he makes it known in every possible way, and for that purpose spends money in a fashion his grandfather fifty years ago would have regarded as astounding extravagance. Salesmanship and advertising are in great part responsible for the spectacular development of all our leading industries, and will continue to open up markets for the new products of tomorrow.

8. *Three great classes of business.* For our present purpose it seems proper to divide business into the following three classes:

First—The production and sale of gods. This kind of business is commonly known as "industry," and embraces, besides manufacturing, the extractive industries: mining, agriculture and lumbering. The individual farmer may not be classed as a business man because of the small scale on which he operates, yet agriculture as a whole is properly regarded as an industry.

Second—The purchase and sale of commodities. By "commodity" is meant anything which has value and is therefore salable. This kind of business embraces all activities of trade and merchandising.

Third—The purchase and sale of services, whether the service of human beings or the use of material things. This class embraces many different kinds of human activity. The banker may be regarded as a dealer in that valuable but immaterial thing called credit, or we may say, without splitting hairs, that the charge he makes when he discounts a promissory note is for the service the bank renders. A theatrical manager who hires the services of players is a business m an, but the players are not. The railroad, steamship, telegraph and telephone companies sell services. The city landlord sells to his tenant the right to use an apartment; strictly speaking, he is selling a service.

This use of the word "service" may seem technical to the reader, but it is not difficult to understand. A man renders you a service whenever he aids you in getting what you want. Any man who makes a "business" of rendering services to others and is looking for a profit and taking a risk, is in business.

9. *The professions*. There are many gainful occupations that are not classed as business for the reason that profit-making is not their primary aim. The most important of these are the professions and the arts. The three best-known professions are law, medicine and theology, often referred to as the learned professions. In recent years, other callings have acquired a claim to rank as professions, as, for example, engineering and architecture.

A professional man finds his reward not merely in the money he earns, which comes to him usually in fees and retainers, but in his love of the work and his sense of its dignity and importance, in his personal independence, in the distinction he achieves because of his skill and intelligence and the respect he commands from his colleagues.

The professions differ from business occupations in that they have definite codes of ethics which prescribe and limit the conduct of practitioners in the various contingencies likely to arise. As is well known, it is unethical for a professional man to advertise, for the only thing he can advertise is his own ability. It is all right for the merchant to extol the virtues and qualities of his goods, or for a druggist to claim that he handles only pure drugs, but it would be in bad taste for a doctor to boast of his wondrous cures, or for the lawyer to brag about his success in the courts.

Members of some professions, however, are wise if they make a study of business problems. Many of our most successful lawyers, for example, are constantly occupied with cases which cannot be thoroughly understood by one who is ignorant of business principles and customs. The engineer or the architect who knows nothing of corporation finance, or business law, or cost finding, will never rise to the highest rank in his profession.

10. *Is business a profession?* If we analyze the so-called learned professions, we find them distinguished by these two characteristics: first, in their practice, brains are far more important than technique or manual skill; second, education in certain sciences is essential to success. No calling deserves to be called a profession if its tasks and problems are so simple as to be within the grasp of any man of ordinary ability and education. The problems of a profession can be correctly solved only by a man who has had thorough training in science.

The physician for example, apart from his knowledge of *materia medica*, must be well grounded in anatomy, physiology, chemistry and bacteriology. Psychology should be added to this list. The well-trained lawyer should be disciplined in the sciences of pure logic and of jurisprudence, in ethics, in the evolution of law and in the theories that explain and justify legal doctrines. When the physician or lawyer is not thus trained, the young lawyer merely knowing the statutes and procedure of his jurisdiction, and the young physician knowing only drugs and symptoms, both are empiricists and do not deserve to be called professional men.

Certain business callings in recent years have risen into the professional ranks. Some years ago, few public accountants would have claimed that their occupation was professional in character. The accountant was then often referred to as a "bookkeeper out of a job." But the really expert accountants know very well that their tasks cannot be performed by the ordinary bookkeeper, that the accountant cannot do his best work unless he knows a great deal about the business man's problems.

It has been largely because of the accountants' belief in the high character of their work that the university schools of commerce train men in all the sciences underlying business as well as in the theory and practice of accounting. For the same reason, many states have passed laws providing that no man shall style himself a "certified public accountant" until he has successfully passed examinations conducted by the state authorities. In view of these conditions, the accountant may fairly claim that his calling has acquired professional standing.

Other business occupations, notably advertising and the work of the credit man, are rapidly moving in the same upward direction. Entrance into these callings is not yet guarded by statute, but many of the leaders already realize the need for superior training, and schools of commerce are doing their best to supply it.

11. *What constitutes success in business?* Since profit is admittedly the aim of business, it would logically follow that a business man's success can be measured only by the amount of money he makes. As a general statement this is perfectly true, yet erroneous inferences and implications are quite possible.

The manager of a New York City bank may raise the net earnings of his bank by one million dollars a year and yet not really be as successful as a small country banker who increases his bank's revenue by only ten thousand a year. In the same way, the business of a city merchant may annually expand by a million dollars, and yet he may be properly regarded as less successful than a small country merchant whose volume of business is increasing at the rate of only ten thousand dollars a year. The city banker and merchant have practically unlimited opportunities of expansion, while the country banker and merchant are hemmed in by the narrow environment. The latter may have done all that could be done to increase business, keep down costs, and increase net revenues.

Suppose that two brothers go into business, one going to the city, the other preferring to remain in the home town. The one in the city has a fortune of a million dollars at the end of twenty years, while the country brother has accumulated only fifty thousand dollars. It would be unfair to conclude that one is twenty times more successful than the other. We must not forget that while profit is the aim of business, men are influenced by many other motives when they choose a business or its location. Money is a tangible reward of a successful business, but money is not everything worth while in life.

To judge wisely, therefore, of a man's success in business, we must know: First, has he accomplished what he set out to do? Second, has the volume of his business been as large as was warranted by its location? And, third, has its management been so sound that profits have been as large as could reasonably be expected?

12. *Dignity and importance of business.* To people who are not well-read in history, it may seem strange that an author should think it necessary to prove that business is an important and worthy occupation. To them it will seem perfectly obvious that business is both important and worthy. Only a generation ago, however, if a boy chose to be a lawyer or a doctor or a preacher, his parents took pride in the fact, and viewed with more or less unconscious pit those friends whose sons had gone into business.

In Europe fifty years ago, business was thought something altogether too vulgar to engage the attention of the nobility, and two thousand years ago, when business was comparatively simple, especially among the Greeks and Romans, business matters were attended either by slaves or by a class of citizens much despised. To devote one's life merely to the making of money was deemed ignoble and unworthy. How much finer to be an orator, a warrior, a poet, a painter or a sculptor!

It would be a waste of time to make comparisons and try to determine whether one calling is finer or nobler than any another. Men are born into the world with different capabilities, and it should be the duty and ambition of each to do that work which he can do best, and to put all his soul into it, whether he write poetry, paint pictures, play the violin, or buy and sell groceries. Then each will deserve respect and honor since each is rendering a community service.

When we consider that the rendering of services to humanity is an essential element of business, and that no business can long be successful if it fails to render such service, we must admit that a great business man deserves honor and respect just as does a great lawyer or physician. The adjective "commercial" cannot be justly used to imply reproach or contempt. To be sure, business may be done in dishonorable fashion. There may be lying, cheating, misrepresentation. But these evils are also found in professions. In the long run, both in the professions and in business, they work against great success. Business as a calling cannot be indicted because some grocer used loaded scales or some broker deceives trusting investors.

Business has made our civilization possible. If we should return to the methods of business in vogue even a few centuries ago, our national wealth would dwindle and disappear. The farmers' great markets would vanish and production would come to a standstill. The debt society owes to business is so obvious and so great that there should be no excuse for an author to devote a page to the discussion of this sort. But there *is* an excuse. It is the ignorant and often vicious hostility to business frequently manifested, and the untrue assumption that our wealth is wholly the creation of farmers and factory workers.

13. *How business creates wealth*. History shows that nations grow rich and their peoples enjoy a high degree of comfort and culture only where the principal occupations are manufacturing and trade. No principally pastoral or agricultural nation has accumulated great wealth or distributed the conveniences of civilization widely among its people. The reason for this state of affairs is a simple one-agriculture does not produce the large amounts needed to provide capital.

Without the large amounts of capital savings accumulated in a manufacturing or trading nation, the really notable technological advances do not get made. It takes money, and a lot of it, to perfect new machines and progress-to take the discoveries of science or the happy inspiration of inventive genius, and from these to perfect the process which gives a new product to the world, or which converts a former luxury into a common article of convenience. Even where it is a simple matter of bringing a widely desired product from another land, it takes capital to build ships, to hire and maintain crews, and to develop the instruments and machines for making navigation safer and swifter.

As a humble example of what capital and machines can accomplish, take the familiar table companion, black pepper-unobtrusively present in the household, free on the counter of the cheapest restaurant. Most people would be surprised to learn that not too long ago pepper was so rare that bitter wars were fought for possession of the pepper lands. Pepper was high on the list of objectives that lured Columbus to set his course for the Indies. The pepper carried back to Europe on the only surviving ship of Magellan's fleet paid for all the lost ships and yielded a profit besides. Men with capital to invest launched more ships, developed steamships to replace the slower clippers, and established the network of wholesale importers and retail outlets that have made pepper as plentiful and inexpensive as anything grown in the local community.

14. *Inventions, and their economic timing*. The world rightly reveres its great inventors and discoverers. Too much

honor can scarcely be paid to these men of genius. Nevertheless, the inventor is helpless unless the times are ripe to receive his discoveries, and unless other men are ready to risk the funds necessary to exploit his ideas and promote their acceptance. That is why so many important inventions have had to be discovered and rediscovered, not once, but many times. It may take decades or even centuries to bring an invention to its commercial fruition.

The case of Hero of Alexandria, who lived in the second century before Christ, will illustrate the point. Hero invented not only one but two steam engines-a primitive model of a steam reaction turbine and an equally primitive pressure engine. Alexandria was a great city, wealthy and enterprising, and a center for scientific research, but the inventions of Hero went unrecognized. Men were not looking for steam power in an age of abundant slave labor.

Neither was the world ready for the steam engine in 1601, when Giovanni della Porta published his plans for one. Just before the century ended, however, an Englishman, Thomas Savery, obtained a patent for a water-raising engine, powered by steam. England, unlike Egypt and Italy, had coal mines from which unwanted water had to be pumped; necessity once again mothered invention. Still, acceptance was slow; fewer than a half-dozen steam engines were in actual service in England prior to 1790. It took the genius of James Watt to show England how efficiently the machine could replace hand tools. Once the demonstration was understood, England changed from an agricultural to an industrial nation, from handicrafts to mass production and worldwide commerce.

15. *Business limitations upon invention*. Not only does the inventor stand in need of other men's capital savings for the funds required to develop and promote his discovery, but he must also consider the full picture of what his invention may involve as a business venture. If he sets up his own company to produce and market his discovery, it will need capital for plant, personnel and equipment. If he sells his patent to an existing company, that company must decide whether it can supply the demand which the invention will create, or whether it must expand, and how much. If the company decides against expansion, and the invention is wanted by more customers than the company can take care of with its present pant and capitalization,

competitors will soon be in the field, with "improved" models to sell.

This matter of considering public demand for an invention can be very serious. It must be kept in view when an investor or a research department is estimating the cost of promoting a new idea. Research creates wealth, but experience shows that a capital investment is required larger than the wealth created. Customers must be taken care of-this is a major law of business; but meeting their demand calls for a capital investment that may mount high. Actually, under present conditions, it is a rare inventor who is able to finance the development of his invention and then finance the company that must be set up to supply the demand his invention may create. Nor can any company manufacture and market all the products and product improvements that an alert research department is able to devise; to try to do so, would hopelessly dissipate its energies and capital. It must concentrate on a few.

16. *Where does business get its capital?* Capital comes either from the savings of others, as made available through lending institutions, or comes from the profits accumulated by a going concern. Thus profit is actually the life-blood of business expansion. In the words of Webster, capital is "an aggregation of economic goods used to promote the production of other goods, instead of being valuable solely for purposes of immediate enjoyment." Capital savings, borrowed from others or accumulated from operating profits, fathers new enterprises or expands old ones, and so creates ever-widening employment and wealth.

In a democracy, where enterprise may be regulated but is essentially free, capital savings are voluntary. Business companies set aside a part of their operating profits as "surplus," other parts for "depreciation" and "maintenance." The precise amounts are at their own discretion. In countries where business enterprise is not free but is wholly directed by the government, capital savings may be forced not only on business but also on the population as a whole.

Japan and soviet Russia offer two conspicuous examples of enforced savings to get capital for industrial expansion. In prewar Japan, the method was to keep workers' incomes very low and to allow high profits to great industrialists, who promptly reinvested their profits for business. Japan wanted steel and armament plants, and the people's welfare had to take second

15

place. The policy was dramatized by the German Nazis in their slogan, "Bullets before Butter." This was a war measure, whereas Japan kept its people living miserably for decades. In either case, the principles and the effects were the same.

Russia, too, in need of funds for buying mill and railroad equipment from abroad or for producing machinery at home, has kept the living standards of its people at a low level. Each Five-Year-Plan has been a new program of popular expropriation, enforced for the purposes determined by the Kremlin. The necessity of patriotism of the method is not here in question; we are interested only in the noting that capital savings, voluntary or enforced, are necessary for economic progress, even under communism.

17.*Why business needs more capital, and still more.* It is the advent of the machine that has compelled business to seek larger amounts of capital than were ever thought necessary before. The Age of the Machines was only in its infancy when the thirteen colonies formed the United States of America. There were few factories, few good roads, no railroads nor steamships, very little machinery of any sort. Newspapers were broadsheets printed on hand presses and read by candle light. It was still true, as men had always believed, that "labor is the source of all wealth."

The progress of the Machine Age changed all that. Economists estimate that the electric power now generated in the United States does the work of half a billion men working eight hours a day-many times the entire working population of the nation. Machines do almost anything, from carrying a message across the seven sea at incredible speed to building a battleship in the fewest possible operations. Machines, and the science to back them, are now the true source of wealth.

But machines cost money, can be had only if the business has the necessary capital. A few tears ago, a neighborhood grocery store could be equipped with simple shelving and counters, and stocked on a relatively small capital investment. Today, even the small store must be equipped with refrigerators, frozen food bins, and, preferably, modern display cases of several types. Electric grinders, improved weighing machines, and cash registers are other items that must be bought. Papa and mamma, with the aid of the kids, may still run the store as of yore, but the store is considerably different-and more expensive. Stocks are more varied.

The case of manufacturing business is much more complex. The business may be small to start with, but the men who are launching it invariably take pride in having the latest and best machinery. In an increasing number of industries, it is not even possible to make a start without a large capital investment, as, for example, in petroleum refining, aluminum manufacturing, or rayon production. The same situation is arising in agriculture, which is rapidly becoming mechanized. Tractors, combines, planters, cultivators, sprayers, cutting and picking machines save thousands of man-hours of hard labor, but at a price. The price, of course, is a substantial amount of capital.

18. *But capital is not everything.* In and of itself, capital is inert and sterile. It may be an indispensable means, but it remains only a means, requiring the direction of human intelligence and enterprise. Two business men may start out with the same amounts of capital, but one may fritter his away in unprofitable bypaths, missing the main highway to success. That is why, despite the large amounts of capital needed in many industries, there is always room for the, an imbued with the spirit of enterprise. New machines and new applications of science may close some doors because of their initial expensiveness, but they open other doors through the by-products and accessories they create.

The truth that capital without enterprise is dead may be illustrated from the curious case of India, much of whose capital is in the primitive form of cattle. As every schoolboy wrestling with Latin knows, the word "capital" is derived from the Latin "caput," meaning head, and referring especially to the heads of cattle. In earlier ages, cattle were wealth and used as money. To know how wealthy a man was, you merely counted his cattle.

Now India, according to this primitive standard, should be wealthy, for it has more cattle than the next five or six cattle-holding countries-more than three times as many as the United States, more than ten times as many as its neighbor to the east, China. One would expect to find the most profitable dairy and meat industry in India. But no, the Hindu religion makes the cow a sacred animal, to be venerated but not butchered. The cattle are left underdeveloped and produce little milk, and that low in fat content. The result is that Indian consumption, both of milk and of beef, is the lowest of any large population, and he Hindus of India are perhaps the most poorly nourished of any people in the world. Moreover, the expense of maintaining their useless herd of cattle is keeping the Indians poor. Per capita income is the lowest of any large country.

19. *To enterprise, add organizing and execute ability.* If the spirit of enterprise is required to make capital fruitful, so are the abilities to organize and to direct the business mechanism needed to achieve the purposes for which capital has been secured. Whenever a business is large enough to require more than one worker, division of labor comes into play and the need of organization and executive ability becomes at once evident. With the growth of the business, departments must be set up, new routines evolved, operating costs balanced with market opportunities. Planning, research, advertising, salesmanship must all be provided for, along with the inevitable accounting and financing.

Men of managerial caliber are not too abundant, and those with special gifts along executive lines are not only in demand but are constantly being requisitioned by the companies that need their services. The larger companies are able to offer larger rewards and consequently often lure the ablest managers from the smaller companies. A small company headed by a gifted executive is not likely to remain small for long-a fact that large competitors appreciate fully. If, as happens now and then, a large company plods along under mediocre management, it may find itself outdistanced by competitors no longer small.

Unexpected confirmation of the importance of organizing ability is afforded by the experience if nations which have substituted state capitalism for free enterprise. Soviet Russia, for example, has had to reward its managers of industry by larger salaries, better housing, and other inducements. The cooperatives of Sweden, Denmark and also the United States have learned that even under "industrial democracy" it pays to spend money for managerial ability.

20. *Opportunities for the business executive.* None of the many changes taking place in the world's economic life appears likely to diminish the opportunities open to the man gifted with executive ability and trained in business administration. He is wanted everywhere-in communistic Russia, in socialistic Sweden, in democratic America. The complexities of machine production have only increased the demand for his services.

What is important is the attitude of the young man in business and the vision that animates his efforts. Is his present work merely a "job" to him-a disagreeable routine in which he sees no future? The typical man with a "job" is very much given to thinking that he is overworked and underpaid, and to complaining about the big salaries paid to the men above him.

The trouble with men of this kind (unfortunately, they are numerous), is that they do not know what business means, cannot see the possibilities in their work nor how to make it help their progress upward. There is a sense in which every business "job" is a gold mine. The man who works for the gold in the job rather than for the money in the pay envelope, is the fellow who gets on. He knows that he is learning the A,B, C's of business, no matter how humble his work.

But the man who starts low down the ladder need not drudge all his days. Business is much more than a "job"; it is, in reality, a fascinating game. Analyze any popular game-baseball, tennis or golf-and you will find that there is a great deal of downright work performed in each. It would be called work if performed outside the game. What turns all this effort into a pleasure? Three circumstances appear to explain the change: first, the number of obstacles in the way of a successful play; second, the joy the human animal takes in triumphing over obstacles, particularly if at the same time he proves himself the better fellow; third, the freakish behavior of the Goddess of Chance, which adds surprise to the game at every turn.

All these game elements are found in business, and your real business man, if he is in good health, gets as much pleasure out of his day's "work" as he ever did out of any game he played as a boy. That is why he is so often tempted to stay in active business too long, when the need for staying has passed.

Add to these considerations the fact that business, if rightly pursued, not only makes for personal happiness but mightily aids the progress of society. It conceives most of the ideas which make for better living and puts these ideas into practical form. Business supplies the needs and comforts of peacetime and the munitions to defend the nation in time of war. Pursued with intelligence and integrity, business is worthy of the best talents of any man.

Business and Social Progress

1. *The business man appears early.* The contributions of business to social progress began early-as soon, in fact, as history itself began. Even before there was any recorded history, the business man was making himself known, supervising the transportation of raw materials and hand-wrought articles from one land to another and exchanging products and materials on a barter basis. The many imported articles dug up by the archaeologists are mute evidence of prehistoric commerce.

Oral tradition, afterwards reduced to writing, offers other confirmation. Thus, the heroes of the Greek Iliad and the Norse saga appear in poetic legend wearing armor and brandishing weapons which neither they nor their henchmen knew how to make-weapons which must have been supplied by wandering traders from the more advanced civilizations of the Near East.

It appears likely that the ancient business man had a prominent hand in the invention of writing, thereby making records and history possible. Writing was not invented all at once, and alphabetic writing did not come until after centuries of experimentation with rude pictograms. No class in ancient society needed records more than the merchants whose donkey and camel caravans pioneered the first trade routes between the Euphrates and the Nile, or between the Euphrates and India. Bills of lading, contracts, instructions to drivers and agents had to be improvised somehow, and this necessity must have spurred the development of picture-notation into a system based on a crude alphabet. Certainly, the legal documents of the business and are practically as old as the inscriptions wherein kings and princes boasted of their victories and conquests.

2. *The first business civilization.* The mud flats of the Tigris-Euphrates delta, in Mesopotamia, were the scene of the world's first business civilization. It was the land which contained, among other cities, the Ur where the Hebrew patriarch Abraham spent his boyhood, and from which he set out to find a new home and fortune in the West. Abraham preferred the wide

open spaces and the life of a cattle and sheep baron to the bustling commercial life he left behind in Ur.

From Ur and a dozen cities which the Sumerians had built upon the Euphrates delta, plodded the caravans of donkeys and camels laden with bronze weapons, metal ornaments, fine cloth, drugs and dyes-all manufactured by the skilled hands of the Sumerian artisans. Across the deserts and uplands to Syria and Egypt, on to the west, and to Iran and even India, on the east, the caravans carried all their wares to be exchanged for the spices, medicinal bark, silver, copper, and gems of the East and West. There was no trade in the bulk goods needed by the mases, for a very large caravan would be required to transport as much as a hundred tons. Caravan trade was luxury trade; its goods had high value relative to their bulk.

The record-keeping for Sumerian trade was done on the material that was most plentiful, namely, clay. Contracts, letters of credit, leases and court orders were engraved on clay tablets, baked hard in the sun, and stored in temple jars or office vaults. Coined money did not appear for centuries, but precious metals were shaped into bars and stamped with the guaranty of some temple or its deity. Partnerships were entered into or were dissolved by written documents, sealed and attested by regular courts. The priests of the large temples were organized into corporations, and extensive workshops under the direction manufactures commercial products from the offerings of worshippers and the tithes of tenants who had leased temple-owned lands. Even the gods were business men in Sumer.

The records of a weaving shop attached to a temple in Ur have been preserved and show how carefully the temple managers kept their accounts. Twelve kinds if woolen cloth were being made in this workshop in the twentieth century B.C. The employees were all slaves, and women-so many to a room, directed by overseers. St the beginning of each month was recorded the amount of raw wool issued to each worker and at the month's end the weight of each cloth which the worker had woven. Allowance was made for unavoidable waste in the process of manufacture according to a percentage worked out by the temple managers.

In parallel columns, on the same clay tablets, were itemized the supplies issued to the women workings during the month in lieu of wages-items like bread, cheese and meat. A final column showed the net profit or loss, per worker, for the month. Other tablets summarized the workshop's progress over longer periods. In a city like Ur, with at least a quarter million inhabitants and famous for its textiles, there must have been hundreds of workshops, large and small, managed with the same businesslike care.

3. *Business and social progress in Sumer.* The twentieth century B.C. is a long distance form the twentieth century A.D., but even so, the contributions made by business to social progress in that earlier century are typical of what business has been accomplishing ever since. Thanks to the hot dry sands which preserved the clay tablets of the Sumerian business man, we have a better picture of his accomplishments than of those of many centuries nearer to our own.

First of all, as one might expect, the standard of living in Sumer was higher than in neighboring countries where agriculture or cattle-raising was dominant. This standard was higher for the nobles, priests, and government officials, but the middle class of traders, professional men and free farmers participated in it to some degree. The disagreeable and hard labor was done by slaves, Sumerian or foreign-born, as was inevitable before men had learned how to utilize animals for power or to devise machines. But the Sumerian slave could engage in business on his own account, accumulate money, and buy his freedom; in general, he was much better treated than slaves elsewhere.

Women, too, usually accorded few rights in ancient societies, were liberally provided for in Sumerian law. They could own money without interference from Friend Husband, could engage in business independently, could appear in court on an equal footing with men. If her husband were away on a long trip, the wife was allowed to manage his affairs and take a third of any profits for herself.

These liberal attitudes toward slaves and women are fairly typical of all ancient civilizations in the business man was the prominent figure; they decidedly were not present, the historians tell us, in states exalting the warrior above all figures, or in states devoted almost exclusively to agriculture. The explanation appears to be twofold. The wife assisting her husband in business meets the public, must often act as his agent; consequently, needs a higher level status than a farmwife. Again, the trader, visiting many countries and comparing varied customs, acquires a tolerance of viewpoint and a willingness to depart from tradition not easily acquired by the squire that sticks to his land.

The same attitudes of tolerance and broadmindedness led the ancient man of business to advocate many social reforms, and often to take a critical stand respecting political and religious traditions. Science, both theoretical and applied, was welcomed in the business civilization, and so was philosophy, the mother of the sciences. It was in another business civilization, the Greek city Miletus, that a business man named Thales became the father of philosophy.

Finally, the ancient business man was instinctively a pacifist. He might engage in the armament trade, but he did not desire to promote war at home. In fact, he was inclined to underrate the chances of war and to let his defenses grow weak. That happened in Sumer, in the twentieth century B.C. when the Babylonian Hammurabi conquered Sumer with a minimum of resistance. The Sumerian business men had seen what was coming, had preferred to give up their nominal independence rather than suffer destruction in a great war. Not so lucky were some of the other business civilizations-the Lydians, the Sybarites, the Etruscans, the Carthaginians. They, too, were envied by the restless warrior nations, but were unable to repel or to make terms with them.

4. *Feud between the warrior and the business man.* One of the saddest pages in history is the story of the feud between the warrior and the business man, a feud which delayed and interrupted social progress and destroyed untold economic values. One unfortunate result of this feud, moreover, was the prejudice created through the slanders of the conquering warriors, who had an unpleasant way of wiping out libraries and archives as well as business establishments and residences, so that no record might remain to refute their report on the victims.

The much-respected Greeks and Romans began as warriors and pirates, destroying and slandering as they went along. The "heroes" of Homer, for example, were robber barons plundering one another or lying in wait for the merchant ships that traded out of Sidon and Tyre-two Phoenician cities on the coast of Asia Minor that were far in advance of the as yet rude Greeks. The latter saw the advantage in attacking the Phoenicians were crafty, prone to cheat them in barter and to steal their daughters for sale in the slave markets. The Greek warriors who made a business of plundering were termed *peiratai*, or pirates, a term of respect meaning adventurers. Troy and Corinth, two of the earlier Greek cities, began as pirate nests, and the famed King Minos was a robber baron living on what he could take from the Phoenicians.

The pages of Homer celebrate the exploits of these pirate heroes-warriors with a strong sense of caste who had learned despite the merchant as a man "with a memory for his freight" and "greedily gotten gains." When a courtier wanted to insult the rescued Odysseus, he suggested that the half-drowned stranger might be a merchant. Odysseus met this slander by hurling a monstrous stone a great distance, thereby proving himself a warrior and at once gaining admission to the banquet hall where the heroes were feasting.

The feud between merchant and warrior continued to the end of Greek history, and beyond. Those Greek cities on the coast of Asia Minor which followed the example of their Asiatic neighbors and took up commerce in a big way, were reproached by the mainland Greeks as unmanly and immoral. In the end, they were wiped off the map or reduced to obscurity. The prejudice against the business man was kept alive even in Athens, the center of the highest Greek culture. Foreign trade was carried on by foreigners who had to live outside the walls of Athens and were denied citizenship. Plato, blue-printing the ideal republic, consigned the business man to a level with cobblers and masons. In the Laws, a citizen was to be punished if he engaged in business.

5. *What the Romans destroyed*. The Roman's began as hardy rustics who scorned the comforts and gadgets of the trader cities. The merchant-princes of Sybaris (from whom the world's first cookbook seems to have come) were despised as degenerates. Even more scorned were their Etruscan neighbors of northern Italy, although the Romans first borrowed such advantages as paved streets, sewers and aqueducts before destroying these neighbors. From them, moreover, the Romans took core ideas for military organization and a legal system; also, the symbol of the axe-and-bundle Fasces, the purple-bordered toga, and the custom of a "triumph" after a victory. In return, the Romans blasted the Etruscans so completely that only in our time have scholars been able to rehabilitate the Etruscan civilization and to reveal the great debt of the Romans to it. But the perfect demonstration of Roman ruthlessness was reserved for Carthage.

Across the Mediterranean from Italy, on the Gulf of Tunis, stood the greatest of the trader cities, Carthage. It had a population of more than 700,000. Its wide commerce and many colonies and trading-posts made Carthage an empire, but it was an empire, but it was an empire ruled by business men, owning no allegiance to king or pontiff. Nothing like it was seen again until the rise of the Dutch sea-cities, in the seventeenth century A.D. Unlike the Greek cities whose constitutions were studied by Aristotle, Carthage enjoyed a stability of government that amazed the inquiring philosopher. Aristotle concluded that what kept the people so free from revolutions or dictatorships was the high standard of living made possible by Carthaginian commerce.

Contented and envying none, the Carthaginians had no warrior class but hired what soldiers were needed for police duties. After the Romans began their wars against them, the Carthaginians were to regret their lack of military training; not even the genius of a Hannibal could make up for the want of native warriors imbued with the fighting spirit. Hannibal was given an army of mercenaries, great five-decked ships, herds of elephants, and technical equipment in profusion, but these were not enough, even though war was carried into Italy itself. Eventually, the Romans laid proud Carthage low, destroying its libraries along with everything else, and sowing salt in its ruins. In the same year, they administered the same treatment to Corinth, the commercial metropolis of the eastern Mediterranean.

How much of good and how much of evil was wiped out by the merciless warrior-landlords of Rome no can say, but the business man did not recover his old position of influence for centuries. Alexandria, Rhodes, and Palmyra were all occupied by the Roman legions. Sheep grazed in the ruins of many a commercial center; whole nations were plunged into poverty to make a Roman holiday. As long as Rome stood, the business man was kept subordinate, although the land-holding patricians were not above making a fortune out of tax-gathering or munitions contracts. And although Rome itself grew to be a great metropolis, it was a political metropolis, not an industrial one. It was a seat of government: first, for the Roman empire; second, during the Middle Ages, for the Christian church.

6. *The business man under the Church*. Christianity took hold first among the workers of the cities; the rural folk (the *pagani* from which the word "pagan" comes) held fast to the older religions. The city workers, whether freedmen or slaves, were poor and oppressed; the gospel of the divine carpenter who had scrounged the money-chargers from the temple made an instant appeal to them. And the primitive Church took a special care of the downtrodden who came to it as a refuge.

At first, the Christian brotherhoods held all their goods in common, setting any surplus aside for the aid of the poor. The clergy were forbidden to trade. Middlemen and money-lenders were condemned by the Church Fathers, who regarded the taking of interest on loans as sinful usury. The business man was regarded with suspicion, as the willing dupe of avarice.

The success of Christianity in becoming the official religion of the Roman Empire brought about a modification of these attitudes. The Church took over pagan temples, including their many business enterprises. Business men were numbered among the faithful; many gave wealth to the Church or bequeathed endowments. Merchants accompanied missionaries to the heathen people of northern Europe, helped the Church to organize governments and commerce for the barbarian converts. The monasteries became important producing and trading centers.

Despite these developments, the Church did not altogether relax its primitive attitude toward property and finance. Money-lending was restricted to the Jews during most of the Middle Ages; a feudal society of landholding nobles and prelates had scant appreciation of the functions of capital and credit. Nevertheless, the medieval merchants organized the foundations of the future commerce, developed towns and free cities, fostered handicrafts, conducted markets and fairs, built up a sea trade with the Levant, and transported the Crusaders who tried to wrest Palestine from the Moslems.

By allying themselves with the kings, whose authority was only n0minal as long as Europe was ruled by thousands of petty nobles, the business-minded towns helped to undermine the feudal system and supplant it with centralized national governments. The towns were willing to pay taxes and so finance the kings, in return for royal protection against the exactions of the nobles, many of whom were scarcely to be distinguished from freebooting pirates. With financial backing, the king built roads, transported troops, maintained garrisons, civil governments, and messenger service-all necessary for centralized administration. The feudal lords were either kept within bounds or transformed into courtiers, living under the eyes of the king.

7. *The Age of Discovery.* The early triumphs of discovery and exploration after 1400 were pioneered by individuals like Prince Henry the Navigator and Christopher Columbus, but the systematic exploration of the discoveries in the Atlantic and the Pacific was the work of business organizations like the Dutch and English East Indies Companies, formed around 1600. These joint stock companies solved the problem of how to gather the large amounts of capital needed for the founding of a Virginia or a Massachusetts, or for the commercial exploitation of India or Malaya.

The operations of the stock companies also speeded up the development of credit and banking, which during the Middle Ages had been developed to any large extent only in Italy. In England, the goldsmiths (to whose strong-boxes people entrusted their valuables) gradually built up a business in discount and deposits. Instead of letting the cash entrusted to them lie idle in their vaults, they lent it to other business men and to the ever needy kings. In Germany, the Fugger family, through shrewd loans and high interest, built up a "money-power" unparalleled since the days of the Roman Caesars. The business of the Fuggers extended from Poland to Spain, from Antwerp to Naples. Unfortunately, it was purely a family affair, depending upon the transmission of business genius from father to son, and the Fugger empire fell apart in the third generation. The secret of permanent corporate organization was not to be discovered for another two centuries.

Meanwhile, first at Antwerp, then at London and elsewhere, the business men of the sixteenth and seventeenth centuries worked out a new way of facilitating the transfer of capital. The new method was to set up a bourse or exchange, where loanable capital was collected and distributed without the use of actual gold or silver. A bourse or exchange was possible only when the volume of trade had reached a high point, indicating how rapidly Europe was becoming business minded during the Age of Discovery.

The exchange was a great convenience. Merchants or princes who formerly would have sought financial aid from private bankers like the Fuggers, could now find the needed capital at Antwerp or Lyons or London. By turning to the exchange, a

French king could and did borrow money of a Turkish pasha. Payments amounting to a million crowns were made in a single morning. The exchanges were just as useful to people with money to save and invest, especially after the shares of the trading companies were put on the market. The stock exchange was, in fact, the natural companion-in-arms of the stock company. It was also a place where investors, patriotic or just plain shrewd, could buy shares in the national debts that were now beginning to mount up. Finally, the exchange was international, trading in foreign as well as domestic shares. Thus, much of the money needed to rebuild London after the fire of 1666, and a large part of the capital of the Bank of England, was subscribed by Dutch investors on the Amsterdam exchange. These same Dutch investors put their money impartially into the Dutch and the English East Indies companies, thereby helping to develop more than one colonial empire.

These empires paid big dividends, both in cash and in produce. Spices, tea, sugar, silk, cotton, and slaves were a few of the leading cargoes carried back from the colonies and sold for a high profits. More important from the standpoint of Europe's commercial growth were the huge imports of Gold and Silver, especially from the colonies of Spain and Americas. The flow of silver from Peru and Mexico, giving Europe more of this medium of exchange than it had ever had before, stimulated a rise in prices that continued for a century and a half. Rising prices made for greater profits, offered the enterpriser countless opportunities, released energies that effected a revolution in production and created the industrialized world we know today.

8. *The Industrial Revolution.* The inventions and experiments that led, first, to the use of steam power to do the work of the world, and, second, to the harnessing of electrical power, literally transformed the physical appearance of city and country in all the industrial nations. What the industrial use of atomic power may do remains to be seen, but there is reason to expect that it will work some radical changes.

As it stands, however, the world of today is so different from what it was in earlier centuries that it is hard for us to feel any intimate kinship with our forefathers. This sense of remoteness from our past could not have existed before the Industrial Revolution. The rate of progress was then slower, and men looked backward as much, if not more, than forward. Why should they not feel at home with their past? Most changes were merely changes of detail or ornamentation.

Very different were the changes that followed upon the Industrial Revolution. These were changes of principle, breaking almost completely with the past. One radical change led to another, and the mass production techniques of our decade differ essentially both from handicrafts and from earlier factory methods.

The wealth created by the new production has raised and broadened the standard of living, stimulating the aspirations of all classes and all peoples. Nations once content to go along on a purely agricultural economy are no longer satisfied with being exporters of raw materials and importers of the products made from those same materials-made by other peoples, at a price, then shipped back to them. These nations want to produce for themselves, set themselves up on an industrialized basis, and so become as modern as the most modern.

9. *Business and the support of science.* Science, pure and applied, made possible the technological advances of the past century and a half. We would be indeed ungrateful not to acknowledge and to pay tribute to the men of science and the inventors who discovered the underlying physical and chemical principles making possible the dynamo, the telephone, the airplane, the Diesel engine, the countless miracles of electronics and plastics. Without the knowledge of fundamental principles, none of these applications of science could have come into existence.

The process of utilizing a discovery in pure science or fundamental research, as it is better called, is often a long and costly one. Thus, it probably cost only a few thousand dollars to support the work of Michael Faraday in his discovery of electro-magnetism, but it took thirty years and the combined work of many inventors, where support must have cost around a million dollars, to perfect a commercially usable dynamo. Add to this the capital required to develop all the other instruments and machines needed in a modern power plant, as well as to extend distribution lines and facilities over a great industrial area, and you get the idea of what a single discovery in fundamental research may lead to, and how necessary becomes the support of business for its full exploitation.

Historically, the university has been the home of pure or fundamental research, and the source from which industry derived its original impetus to research, as well as most of its trained research personnel. Today, fundamental research is being conducted almost as extensively in the great research centers of private industry as in the universities. Trade associations, setting up facilities at their headquarters for cooperative research, have helped to solve the problems of the smaller company unable to finance an extensive research program of its own. In all, the investment of private business in research has passed the billion dollar mark in the United States alone, and keeps growing.

In addition, private business has for many years subsidized much of the scientific research being carried on at the universities and technical institutes. The universities themselves, and the foundations for studying the world's social problems-medical, educational, economic and sociological-have been showered with endowments and gifts from business men who wanted to help their fellows. If, as every thoughtful person must admit, we are living in an age of science, a substantial part of the credit for that accomplishment must be awarded to the business man.

10. *Business and the standard of living*. Throughout history, the great trading and industrial civilizations have enjoyed higher standards of living than existed in the other nations around them. In part, this has been due to the superior ability of trade and industry to raise the per capita income of any people, to create more wealth more rapidly. In addition, a trading people is more demanding, and more inventive.

Business men have long been students of people's wants; were they not, they would create few markets and sell only a fraction of the potential markets they do have. It is to the interest of the trader to stimulate a desire for a higher standard of living, to encourage people to rise above their present level of comfort. As a result, the citizens of a business civilization are likely to be both more restless and more ambitious than are those of an agrarian civilization.

The point was well illustrated in medieval Europe, where the citizenry of the towns attempted and often succeeded) in rising from poverty to positions of affluence, whereas the peasants on the lands of the nobles were not only more likely to remain poor all their lives, but were even forbidden to wear the clothing and ornaments not proper to their social class. If such a ban existed in the towns, the citizen who won his way to wealth was given the status permitting him to wear higher regalia. That might mean, as in England, making him a knight or even a baron. Few peasants ever won this status.

The desire of the business man to widen his market influences the standard of living for multitudes of consumers. The more he sells of his product, the more the business enterpriser must produce. Quantity production brings down the cost; new methods and new machines do the production job still more cheaply.

Year by year, through lowered costs and the impact of competition, a product which originally was a luxury item for the few becomes a staple for the many.

The automobile, and especially the closed car, is a good example of this process of broadening the market. Prior to 1912, the automobile was manufactured chiefly for the wealthy; after 1912, for the so-called middle class of consumers. From 1916 on, the automobile was priced low enough so that increasing numbers of people with relatively modest incomes could own one, aided, further, by the introduction of installment selling. Luxury types of cars continued to be made and sold to the wealthy, of course, but most manufacturers saw the advantage in mass markets, and catered to them.

11. *Utopia begins to take shape*. Considering the sad condition of the world torn by war and wrestling with war's aftermath, it may appear unrealistic in the extreme to say that some of the specifications for Utopia have been realized, and even surpassed, in our century. Nevertheless, such is the case, as any one can see for himself by examining the record.

Utopia, coined by Sir Thomas More as the name for his imaginary ideal state, has come to stand for all the pictures of ideal commonwealths drawn by poets and philosophers from Plato to Edward Bellamy. Most famous of these social blueprints are Plato's *Republic*, More's *Utopia*, Bacon's *New Atlantis*, and Bellamy's *Looking Backward*. They all portray commonwealths peopled by men of generous good will, content to share everything in common, and disclaiming social privileges. The happy citizens of these states live leisurely, have an abundance of the necessaries of life, enjoy the advantages furnished by ingenious gadgets. The particular gadgets for any particular

Utopia depend upon the imaginativeness of the author. In that respect, Francis Bacon was especially prolific, providing his New Atlantis with a central research society, or Solomon's House, equipped with "experimental houses" of many kinds.

In the eyes of many foreign peoples, and measured by most material standards, the United States has in our time approached the Utopian ideal. Its citizens have not, it is true, become ideal Utopian characters, and it has not wiped out poverty. Nevertheless, a larger proportion of the total population lives in comfort than in any previous civilization. The forty-hour week gives the leisure contemplated by most Utopian authors. Necessaries have been provided to a degree that appears wasteful to the average European, and the amusements, access to knowledge, and mastery over time and space surpass anything the Utopians imagined.

The developments predicted for the atomic age will project these materials gains still farther. Whether human nature will take on Utopian traits at the same rate is more questionable. But the material basis is fast being provided; that much is certain.

12. *Idealism in material achievements*. Some critics are inclined to scoff at the business man's stress upon material progress, and even to hold his enthusiasms up to scorn. This attitude is short-sighted and shows an ignorance of the motives behind the invention of material improvements, and underlying even their enjoyment.

The development of the automobile to the level where almost anyone could own one, furnished thousands of families with a means of seeing other regions, visiting with distant relatives and friends, obtaining medical aid or transacting other important business quickly. Compare the American farmer with the European peasant, the latter for centuries bound to his farm and village, poorly educated and informed, expecting little and getting it. His cultural advancement has been definitely retarded by his isolation.

The American farmer, by contrast, enjoys a mobility of movement, thanks to his car or truck, that is as individual as himself. To travel thirty miles by horse and buggy used to take him a whole day; with his car or truck, he covers the same distance in an hour. The equipment of his farm and home, the appearance and mental outlook of his wife and children, all show the effects of easy access to better shopping and education centers.

The wish to provide wife, children and self with a better life, intellectual as well as material, is a form of practical idealism deserving of respect, not scorn. The same motive explains much of the interest of other people everywhere in the acquisition and enjoyment of the applications of science to the business of living. And no little part of the satisfaction which the business man gets from his labors lies in his appreciation of the human aspirations involved in every sale, or potential in the perfecting of every product.

Between world war I and World War II, various visitors to the United States from Europe commented sadly upon our supposed "obsession for tangible and material accomplishment." Within a few years, when the Nazi war machine had subjugated most of the European continent, these same critics pinned their hope for liberation upon America's ability to produce weapons and munitions in overwhelming quantities. The miracle of production was accomplished, but the motives that fired the production effort were an idealistic love of freedom and fair play and a deep hatred of tyranny.

The spirit behind America's material triumphs has been eloquently stated by a former president of the Chamber of Commerce of the United States, Eric A. Johnston. "Most Americans feel in their bones," he says, "that in our country material accomplishment has in it strong elements of idealism and even spirituality…. Hill building railroads, Carnegie smelting steel, Ford providing cheap automobiles for the masses, millions of men nurturing a business or a farm, feel that they are taking part in a larger process-the process of shaping our American civilization….Tangible things do not dominate us-we dominate tangible things, bend them to our will, force them to yield libraries, schools, theaters, philanthropies, larger measures of health and comfort for millions of human beings."

Much more could be written about the contributions of business to social progress, but essentially they boil down to what Mr. Johnston has said on behalf of his fellow business of the United States. The spirit of enterprise, as we have seen, is not a monopoly of any one people, nor of any one age, but has existed from the beginning of recorded history. Making many blunders, sharing the limitations of each successive age, the business man has struggled upward through the centuries, combining individual with social aims, material with idealistic motives. Grave as many be his faults, he has labored, by and large, to bring the good life to more and more people, and to establish lasting peace and a genuine democracy.

Advisory 2

Profit Motivation

1. *Profit as an economic motive*. Throughout history, the hope and expectation of making a profit has been the most powerful incentive to economic advancement. This motive does not appeal to all men, since it carries with it the chance of failure. Profits are not fixed in advance, as are salaries and wages. They may be high, or low, or non-existent, depending upon whether the business is a success or a failure. If the business meets with some degree of success, profits are what is left over for the owners after all expenses have been paid. No one can say what this excess over cost will be in any given year.

Because working for profits entails a risk, the multitude of men prefer working for wages. They are able to do so, however, only because the profit motive has first created wage-paying jobs. To the adventurous few who are willing to take a business chance-to assume the risk of success or failure-economists have applied the term entrepreneur, or enterpriser. These are the men who start new business, launch new products upon an uncertain market, assume collectively the task of industrial expansion.

Some measure of adventurousness is required, also, in the management of the established enterprise. Being established does not free the enterprise from the factor of risk. Profits are the most variable item on a company's balance sheet. Sales may drop off, unexpectedly and even unaccountably, without a corresponding reduction in operating costs. Certain elements of expense either remain fixed, or can be reduced only gradually. Under some circumstances, consequently, a drop of only 10 per cent in sales may produce a decrease in profits running as high as 50 per cent.

Nevertheless, despite their uncertainty, profits are earned frequently enough to appear a glittering reward of business enterprise. Impressive figures are collected by the statisticians showing the high rate of mortality in this or that industry, or the percentage of business that will not survive past their first or second year, but these figures rarely deter a man from starting an enterprise upon which he has set his heart. The enterpriser who is convinced of the merit of his product or service is quite willing to gamble on his ability to succeed against all obstacles.

2. *Who are influenced by the profit motive?* The lure of profit is evident enough in the case of the enterpriser launching a new business, or in the instance of the small business owned by a single individual or by a few partners. What is not so evident is the working of the profit motive in the case of the large corporations, whose owners are the thousands of stockholders scattered over half the globe, having little to do with the actual management of the company. The men responsible for the day-to-day operations are on a salary, perhaps owns no shares in the company. Who, in the corporation, is being influenced by the profit motive in the way that it influences the enterpriser?

Strange as it may seem, it is probable that the managers of a corporation, even though they may not be numbered among its owners, are more profit-conscious than the individual who owns and operates his own business. Profits-and costs-are watched very closely in the corporation. An accounting department collects and analyzes the necessary sales and costs data, then presents the cumulative results weekly or even daily to the managing executives. The latter are practically compelled to follow the curve of rising or falling profits, cannot help becoming cost and profit-conscious. In contrast, the busy owner of a small business can scarcely find time to take his financial soundings-sometimes he does not know where he stands, or how well he is doing, for weeks at a stretch.

It must be remembered, also, that while the managers of a corporation are working for salaries and may or may not own stock, they are keenly aware that their positions and salaries, present and future, depend upon the success of the company in making profits. So, too, the thousands of investors who put their money into the company's stocks and bonds are counting upon continued profits; otherwise, they would not invest.

3. *Profits as a condition for growth*. If a going concern is to thrive, its profits must be more than merely nominal. Breaking even is not enough to pay some return to the stockholding owners of the business, and also to add to the company's capital resources available for the purchase of new equipment, the modernization of old plants, or the building of additional facilities. New inventions and scientific discoveries may call for the scrapping of existing machinery and the installation of new units, for all of which money is required. But the company's savings, if any, come only from its profits-if there are profits. From its undivided profits-the profits not paid to stockholders in the form of dividends-the company takes the capital needed for its improvement and growth.

It is true that companies can and do borrow funds for needed improvements or expansions, either through loans of financial houses or through an approved issue of new bonds to the public. But these loans involve heavy obligations which in turn must be met from profits. Some companies make it a matter of policy to finance improvements from their own earnings. Thus, United States Steel, for a long time the largest corporation in the world and the first billion-dollar company in existence, financed almost all of its huge expenditures for improvements and new construction from its own earnings up to World War II. The owners (the stockholders) had to be content with a market value for their stock scarcely higher than what it had been in 1902, when the corporation was organized.

No company can afford to stand still, unless indeed it has a monopoly, and even then the consuming public, through its government will find ways of enforcing progress. Growth is not only the normal desire of a business enterprise but it is the goal that must be realized if the enterprise is to survive. But growth depends upon new and more capital, which directly or indirectly must come from the company's earned income. Profits, therefore, are both a condition for survival and a test of business efficiency.

4. *Profits are not easily come by*. A fallacy held by too many people outside of business circles is that most enterprises

make huge profits. The larger and more successful the corporation, the more grandiose are the imaginary profits with which uniformed people endow it. Pleasant as it might be for business men if these imaginary profits were only real, the facts must be faced as they are, and they tell an altogether different story.

For example, during the ten years that preceded World War II, from 1030 to 1940, fewer than 50 per cent of all business enterprises in the United States earned a profit. That particular decade included years of depression but it also included some years that were considered good, and the percentage of profit-making enterprises stayed under 50 in good years as well as bad.

The precarious status of business enterprise is authoritatively shown by the data collected since 1900 by Dun & Bradstreet, widely known for their annual listing of credit ratings. Their reference books, covering all types of business concerns except small service enterprises, furnish a reliable guide to what may be termed "vital statistics" of American business. They list business births-new enterprises or new ownerships or new reorganizations. They also list business deaths, whether by simple withdrawals from business, changes in ownership, or outright commercial failures.

Reviewing all these changes back in 1900, Dun & Bradstreet find that one-fifth of the business population undergoes some change annually. Thousands of concerns go out of existence during their first, their second, or their third year, and the average life of a business enterprise is only about sixty-six months. One knows exceptions, of course, running high above the average, as, for example, E.I. du Pont de Nemours & Company, which began its career in a small way in 1802.

Even when a concern survives over a period far above Dun & Bradstreet's sixty-six-month average, it does not follow that its profits are fantastic. Returning to the example of United States Steel, let us examine its consolidated statement for the period of boom, three of depression, and four of about average business.

During those ten years, the company's customers paid in nearly seven billion dollars. The company, in turn, paid out three billion in wages and salaries; another two and one-half billion more in taxes, depreciation and depletion. Of the several billions of income during the decade, there was left a final net income of 472 millions-slightly more than 6.6 per cent of the total receipts, and less than 3 per cent of the company's capital assets. Putting it another way, one out of every sixteen dollars of receipts was paid out as profit to the stockholding owners. These stockholder-owners numbered over 250,000!

5. *The beneficiaries of profits.* If the profits of United States Steel had been somewhat smaller in the decade 1928-38, perhaps only the stockholders would have felt the difference. The employees might have received the same wages and salaries, the government about the same taxes, the suppliers of goods and services their payments. But the stockholders might have gone without dividends for one quarter, or many. Passing up dividends is a familiar story in the business world, oft repeated. The owners of the corporation come last, sometimes wait patiently for years for interrupted dividend payments to be resumed.

It is true, of course, that when dividends are passed up, as in the depression years, wages and salaries are sometimes cut or men are let go. Jobs, after all, depend upon profits and are created by profits. The employee's stake in business profits is a very real one; moreover, it is all the larger form of the fact that the employee is a consumer as well as a worker. Profits invested in newer machines and techniques cut the costs of production and reduce the price of consumers' goods. These reductions directly benefit the employee-consumer.

The history of almost any industry over the past few decades will furnish illustrations of how this process works. Let us take the automobile tires an example. In 1908, the average employee of an American tire maker was being paid 40 cents an hour. He was helping to make a rubber tire selling for $35 and having a life of 2,000 miles. This made the cost 1 ¾ cents a mile. Relating the cost of the tire to the tire worker's wages, the worker had to work half a day (four hours) for every 91.4 miles he drove his car. Few workers owned a car in 1908, and the reason is obvious.

By 1936, the average wage of the tire worker had risen to 88 cents an hour-a gain of 120 per cent. Good as this was, if no other change had occurred, the worker could not have afforded to drive a car. His new wage would have given him only 201.1 tire-miles of operation for half a day's work. But new machines and processes, made possible by capital obtained from profits, had lowered the price of a small tire from $35 to $8 and advanced its operating life from 2,000 miles to about 20,000 miles. Now for half a day's work, the tire company employee could buy the service of four tires for 2,200 miles, and driving a car was economically feasible. Business profits, reinvested in the business, had joined with inventive ingenuity to make possible a tremendous (and greatly appreciated) jump in the worker's standard of living.

The beneficiaries of profits are not individuals only; entire communities share in the rising standards made possible by the accumulation and use of capital to build up or expand business enterprises. Every such expansion means a larger payroll and more purchases of materials and supplies, many of them purchased from suppliers within the community. New employees added to company payrolls contribute their payments for housing, clothing, food, and other personal supplies to the total working capital of the community.

6. *The attack on profits*. Despite the needs of profits for industrial growth, despite their beneficial effects upon individuals and communities and the difficulty with which they are acquired in actual practice, profits have been eyed with suspicion by many persons outside the world of business. Laws against high prices, "usury," and monopolies have appeared in every century, from the most recent to the most ancient. These laws were designed to protect the consumer against the abusive exercise of price-making and profit-taking powers, but price-making and profit-taking as such were not under attack. One prominent exception, of course, was the war conducted by the medieval Church against "usury," that is, against taking a profit on loans.

In our day, the attack has progressed from a war on unfair profits to a campaign against *all* profits. It is profit-making itself that is under attack. Other motives, superior to the profit motive, should stimulate men to produce and distribute, as say the critics. The principal motive adduced as a substitute for the profit motive is that of "service," a motive of dubious force when standing alone.

7. *"Service" as a substitute for the profit motive*. The activities of business result in services rendered, and the business man gets a ken satisfaction from the contemplation of the good he is accomplishing. As we have seen, he is not the

sole beneficiary of business enterprise, nor even the principle beneficiary. A going enterprise, under normal conditions, benefits employees, consumers, other business men, the community and the nation. Consequently, the idea of service is never absent from normal business enterprise, but is, in fact, a genuinely compelling motive.

There is no reason for critics of business to try to separate the motives for profit and service, or worse still, to contrast them as if they were deadly opponents. The two motives can be held by the same man, and actually are. It is the profit motive that leads the business man to plan a launch his commercial enterprise, but it is the service motive that broadens the original motive of profit-seeking to make it fruitful of economic and social good. Business men understand this relationship very well and by and large have lived up to their understanding of it.

To brand the profit motive as selfish and immoral, and to ask that production and distribution be conducted solely from the motive of service, is to ask for what is neither necessary or possible. The one exception to this statement is a time of war or some other calamity endangering the existence of community or nation. In such a time, the service motive is transformed into the patriotic motive, and miracles of production are performed without regard to costs, whether of material or of labor. When peace returns and national danger is less than obvious, appeals to patriotism notoriously meet with less success. The service motive by itself is too vague for the ordinary man to visualize. Just whom is he supposed to be serving, he asks, and why should he toil for them? There may be good answers to these questions, but it is doubtful whether they would have much motivating force.

8. *European experience with substitute motives.* A full eighteen months after the end of World War II, English industry was more seriously disrupted than it had been during the days of the German "blitz." Coal supplies were inadequate to meet the nation's needs, and the government decreed shut-offs of electricity for all but the most essential industries. Four million workers were thrown out of work until more coal, and more electric power, could be obtained. The coldest winter in years added to the general discomfort, and Britons shivered in their homes.

Here was a national crisis, so obvious that it should have spurred work motives of the highest order. How did the coal miners respond? A study of Midland miners at the height of the crisis showed that neither government or private exhortations had brought "the slightest change in the men's habit of taking unauthorized days off." Absenteeism averaged 20 per cent. More than 48 per cent of Midland miners were working fewer than five days a week, although a full working week was still six days. The fact that under Britain's Labor government the coal mines were in process of nationalization appeared to make no difference to miners. Working for the nation did not, of itself, serve as a motive or stimulus to reduce absenteeism and speed up production.

Further investigation disclosed that decidedly material motives were involved in the negative attitude of the miners. What was the use of trying to earn more money, they asked, when the stores were empty and there was nothing to buy? And again, why should anyone work a full week and thereby put himself in a high-tax bracket? As the average miner figured it, he could have more for himself, and live longer, by working and earning less. If the minor's reasoning was not exactly patriotic, it was very human. And it pointed to the need of material motives, corresponding to the profit motive, to stimulate his full productive energies.

Soviet Russia had a similar experience early in its history. In the beginning, the government seized the surplus of agricultural production over the peasants' immediate needs. In a year or two, the surplus disappeared, and the country was in the grip of a terrible famine. The government also seized what factories there were, dispossessing the former owners and replacing the former managers by "technical" committees of Soviet officials. Overhead expenses soared wile production went down. Gradually, Moscow recalled the former managers and instituted a system of special rewards for them.

The conclusion was inescapable that motives of patriotism or service to party were not enough-that if the stimulus of private profit is removed, few are interested in keeping up economic machinery and working it to the best advantage. It might be possible, theoretically, to change human nature through skillful re-education, but as matters stand, special incentives for skill and productivity are an official practice in the Communist economy.

9. *The ethics of competition.* Underlying much of the critical attitude toward the profit motive held by people who are neither Communists or Socialists, is the assumption that there is something wrong about competition-something smacking of the jungle wherein animals prowl about seeking other animals whom they may devour. So much is heard about "unfair competition" that many people, outside the business world, tend to think of all competition as unfair.

Perhaps unconsciously, such persons are really reacting from the extreme doctrines that were popular during the half-century following Darwin's announcement of the theory of evolution. The "struggle for existence" that Darwin found in the plant and animal world was transferred by some popularizers to the human sphere, and finally to the economic scene. Herbert Spencer, whose books had what was then an enormous sale in the United States and Canada, taught that men should keep hands off the progress of nature. Nature will see that the deserving survive the struggle for existence; those who do not survive are the unfit, decreed by nature to be eliminated. This was consoling doctrine to those men who had climbed to the top of the business world, sometimes, unfortunately, by ruthless means. It eased their consciences with regard to those hapless competitors whose elimination they had assisted "nature" to bring about. Finally, it was popular doctrine in the stage of capitalistic evolution in which Britain and America then were, when the former was engaged in empire-building and later in exploiting a continent.

The Spencerian over-emphasis upon the survival of the fittest had long since been abandoned in business theory and, by and large, in business practice. Team-work and cooperation, through trade associations and chambers of commerce, have led another way. Today, it is recognized that the normal man is competitive and cooperative. Cooperation insures a common effort for goals involving common welfare; competition, refereed by trade association or by government, insures the continuous development of improved products and services.

Without competition, the world would take on a monotonous sameness, such as may actually be observed on the streets of Moscow, according to American visitors. No signs, no window displays and no newspaper advertising call attention to the merits of competing products. Blasé consumers who think themselves allergic to advertising, U.S.A. style, would probably

43

soon lose their allergies if they could not get improved products, but had to stand in line for the few models authorized by an all-powerful government.

There is nothing like having an alert, progressive competitor in the same line of business to keep a man on his toes. Your competitor adds and improvement to the product, or works out a more attractive design, or installs new machinery enabling him to cut costs and reduce price a little. Or perhaps he launches a sparkling advertising campaign, or offers dealers better display material. Whatever he does, you must evaluate its effect on your own dealers and customers.

If you judge that the effect is likely to be permanent and serious, you take steps either to emulate him or, if possible, to surpass him. In the end, you find yourself doing what you had supposed to be impossible, with results beneficial to everybody. This is the way in which fair, healthy competition operates; obviously, it is not only ethical but highly desirable.

10. *Doing without competition-and liberty.* In their efforts to blueprint a new kind of economic order in which the disadvantages of the present order would be overcome, socialists of every hue have made much of the slogan, "Production for use." Their idea is that the state should own the machines and operate them for the benefit of everyone. Are hats needed? Very well, count the heads, and make as many hats are there are heads. Then distribute them.

How often shall a man get a hat? And what shall be its quality and style? These are questions for the government to decide, aided, perhaps, by a poll of public opinion. But not necessarily. The government may foresee a war in the offing, and so want to limit manufacturing to armament and munitions. Or it may want to export felt instead of using it for domestic hat-making. In either event, the government may decide to let most of the male population get along a while longer with their old hats, making exceptions only for diplomats, the higher bureaucrats, and the managers of state factories and collective farms. If less important males protest, so much the worse for them. There are ways of dealing with impatient grumblers, especially in an authoritarian state.

If this example appears fantastic, consider what authoritarian nations have done in the recent past. In Japan, under the divine Mikado; in Russia, under the Dictatorship of the Proletariat; In Italy, under the Corporate Fascist State; in Germany, under National Socialism-in all these countries, the common people had their living standards cut down, often dangerously low, in order to provide the state with more funds or materials for war production, or for road-building, or for colonial expansion.

In a totalitarian country, there is no "wasteful" competition among producers of consumer goods; the government decides whether the consumer needs new goods, and how many, and of what quality. Neither are there private profits, except for the government's favorites, and then they are disguised as "bonuses" or subsidies. As long as the economy (usually a war economy) holds up, there is employment for all-on the government's terms. Labor unions never protest these terms, nor go on strike, for they have been incorporated into the state, and are under strict party discipline, like every other group. Newspapers, radio and schools echo with one voice what the government wants the people to be told. There is one, and only one, political party; on the ballot, a single list of names or a place to vote "Yes."

Peoples who have never known free speech or the ballot, and do not understand democratic processes, appear to like authoritarian government, but to those who have had some taste of what democratic liberties and free enterprises are like, nothing can seem more bleak than the state capitalism to which the socialist and fascist regimes appear inevitably to lead. Such capitalism is an ant-hill society on the human level, in which the individual becomes less and less significant. "Wasteful" competition is replaced by "cooperation," but it is an enforced cooperation equivalent to slavery. If history teaches any lesson, or is that freedom and wholesome competition are had together, or lost together.

11. *Improvements of the profit system.* If some peoples are enthusiastic about the benefits of dictatorship, it is because they were neglected or oppressed under previous authoritarian governments, or were the butt of racial or religious hatred. Soviet Russia, for example, appears to have greatly improved the living standards of certain Asiatic nomads and the long-persecuted peoples of the Caucasus, such as the Armenians. Millions of simple people in the Old World, for centuries the victims of tyranny and exploitation, do not understand the

privileges of democracy or the operation of a free economy, but do understand the contrast between the life of the toiling masses and that of a free economy, but do understand the contrast between the life of the toiling masses and that of the privileged few. They understand, also, the tenacity of the few in hanging on to their privileges, and are easily convinced that force alone (the so-called "class struggle") will secure them a share in the good life. The dictator, or the dictatorial party, who promises to use force for the benefit of the many, appears as a benefactor from heaven. Relying on his promises, the peoples, like the Faust of legend, sign away their liberties.

There is a lesson in this for all who believe in the superiority of democracy and free enterprise. That lesson is, of course, that business men must never lose sight of the social effects of their plans and activities-the service motive must reinforce and guide the profit motive. The human consequences need always be visualized, and to do this, business must cultivate and strengthen their powers of sympathetic imagination-a form of imagination of importance.

In point of fact, the lesson of the underprivileged is not a new one to business men. They have steadily extended the area of population enjoying a higher standard of living. Even at the depths of the depressed 1930's, workers in the United States and Canada quite literally had better houses, better clothing, better food, better education, better protection against disease and risk than elsewhere in the world.

It must be granted, nevertheless, that the effort to extend a higher standard of living is incomplete, that not all people have been reached. There are still economic frontiers to be pushed back.

There are also obstacles to competitive enterprise arising from the sad fact that some men will not play the game fairly, but will try to circumvent the law and flout the entire code of business ethics. To control these business mavericks, it is necessary that there be policing by government and by business itself-by government, through such agencies as the Federal Trade Commission and the Interstate Commerce Commission; by business, through trade associations and bureaus to detect fraud or unfair competition.

The job of making democracy more truly democratic, and free enterprise more genuinely free, is a serious task, and never more serious that at this stage in history, when freedom finds itself ringed around by authoritarian influences.

Economic uncertainty and hard times breed dangerous discontents, and one of the most of the difficult problems for free economy to solve is a certain tendency toward recurrent depression and mass unemployment. People do not want to live in the permanent dread of intermittent unemployment and misery. Unfortunately, the freedom to produce, together with the freedom of the consumer to buy or to hoard his savings, make for a natural instability in a free economy. Some countermeasures can be taken, however, where government and business work together, and studies already underway may give us a greater control over the factors producing economic instability, without undue curtailment of freedom.

It should not be thought that the individual business has no part to play in securing economic stability. On the contrary, he has a very important part to play, well expressed by a contemporary business leader in the statement, "The greatest contribution any business man can make toward stability is to operate his business profitably." Recall what profits mean, and who benefits from them, and the truth of this quotation will become apparent at once.

Advisory 3

Business Management

1. *No business can succeed without good management*. If any business is to be profitable, it must be directed by men who understand the principles of good management, and possess the ability to apply those principles to a degree above the average. If the management is *below* average in its understanding and ability the, company will fail. If the management is *only* average, the business may keep going in a routine sort of way but it will not be conspicuous as a profit-maker.

The record of commercial failures shows that poor management, in the judgement of the statisticians, is to blame for around 40 per cent of all failures in business. In reality, the percentage attributable to poor management may be considerably higher, for the commercial records cover only those failures that are openly admitted. Many other concerns wind up their affairs quietly, without the failure becoming a matter of public record. Were these withdrawals from business to be added to the others, the number of failures caused by poor management would probably be a much larger proportion of the total of all failures. It might run higher than 50 per cent.

It is true that few officers of concerns adjudged to have failed because of poor mismanagement had caused their failure.

They would insist that circumstances beyond their control were to blame, that they were bowled over by business conditions which nobody could have anticipated, or that they were the victims of unfair competition or financial juggling. In a few cases, these excuses for failure might be valid; for the overwhelming majority, the excuses would just be excuses, and nothing more.

Business managers who understand marketing and finance do not let themselves become involved in circumstances of a fatal character. They keep up with the indicators of business and economic trends. They test and pretest before they sink money into a new product, a new sales territory, or an ambitious promotion, a new sales territory, or an ambitious promotion campaign. They insist upon having an accounting system that keeps them informed of true inventories and true costs. Every department of the business is required to plan its objectives, sometimes for years ahead, and to operate on a carefully prepared budget.

With all the help that modern business has at its command to chart its course, no management need ever operate in the dark, or run unwarned into hidden snags or unexpected whirlpools. The exceptions to this statement, if in all honesty they are exceptions, will be few indeed, and require investigation. Not even a depression will excuse a management that fails, since many businesses survive to prove that it can be done.

2. *Good management is rarely a one-man affair*. Because success in business requires an understanding of conditions and operations ranging over a wide field-very wide in the case of some companies-it is obvious that one man will rarely have the cyclopedic knowledge for handling all management functions unaided. It is undesirable, in most cases, that he should try to be the entire management, or even a large part of it.

One might think that the beginning stage of a small business would be an exception to this warning against going it alone, but there are legal questions involved (not to mention the choice of product line or service, or of a good location, or of marketing methods) which should have the benefit of expert advice, if at all obtainable. In fact, it is most important to start right than to do anything else that follows, and a right start calls for careful planning and the correct analysis of alternative methods of going ahead.

The failure to seek advice and assistance when it is needed-to make decisions without surveying all the consequences-is perhaps the single greatest single mistake of the manager who leads his business, not to victory, but to bankruptcy. Leadership is good, and often it must be bold, but its true function is to bring out the best efforts of others, and to unite their efforts in a common purpose. In short, good business management is similar to management in athletics-the main job is the building up of a team. Good teamwork is good management.

If it were desirable to reduce good management to a formula, it might run something like this-an alert, fully cooperative team, working toward clearly defined business goals, employing the most efficient methods to achieve those goals. Or, perhaps we might like better the definition of management inscribed on the walls of the Engineering Societies' Library, in New York: "Management is the art and science of preparing, organizing and directing human effort applied to control the forces and utilize the materials of nature for the benefit of man." This definition is inspiring, but it has one drawback-it applies more to the management of production than to the management of finance or marketing, or to the conduct of a service business.

3.*Essential functions of any business*. There are differences of aims, resources and methods to be considered when we pass from one type of business to another. The operating problems of a manufacturing business differ from those of a wholesale or a retail business, and these, again, differ from those of a service business, such as a taxicab company or a laundry. But there are similarities, too-problems that confront the management of all types alike, as, for example, the installation of an efficient system of accounting. Every business needs to know accurately and promptly how well it is doing financially, and what its true costs are. That need is shared in common.

Differences appear when we come to the actual installation of an accounting system. Its forms and classifications will vary from business to business; under ideal conditions, it will be designed expressly to fit a specific business. Operations performed by hand in small concerns will be handled by complicated machines in the accounting departments of large companies. These and other differences will make accounting systems appear quite dissimilar to the uninitiated, yet the same purpose governs all of them-to furnish management with the accurate fiscal control.

Our interest at this point, is to look at the tasks of management common to all, or practically all, types of businesses. To that end, let us examine the following list of essential functions-a list that is meant to be suggestive rather than complete, which the reader may elaborate from his own experience or observation. As it stands, it will suffice to start him thinking about management functions.

ESSENTIAL MANAGEMENT FUNCTIONS

(1) Determining the objective of the business.

    (a) Products, goods, or services to sell?

    (b) Any side-lines or accessory services?

    (c) Classes of customers to reach?

    (d) Any limitations on objectives?

(2) Determining the legal organization.

    (a) Proprietorship?

    (b) Partnership?

    (c) Corporation?

    (d) Legal formalities to be complied with?

(3) Financing the Business.

    (a) How much capital needed?

    (b) Sources?

    (c) Advantageous methods?

(4) Providing a physical plant.

    (a) The right location?

(b) Build or lease?

(c) Equipment needed?

(d) Maintenance?

(e) Insurance and protection?

(5) creating an operating organization.

(a) Production or purchasing personnel?

(b) Sales and advertising personnel?

(c) Office personnel?

(d) Plant maintenance personnel?

(e) Industrial relations and supervisory personnel?

(6) Assembling what the business has to sell.

(a) In a manufacturing business, by production.

(b) In a wholesale or retail business, by purchase.

(c) In a service business, by assembling equipment and workers.

(7) Finding and inducing customers to buy.

(a) Market surveys, research, testing?

(b) Advertising: what kinds?

(c) Salesmanship: What kinds?

(d) Cooperation with distributors?

(e) Consumer contacts for service improvement?

(8) Granting credit and making collections.

(a) Credit and discount policies?

(b) Collection policies?

(9) Setting up accounting controls.

    (a) Customer's accounts-well handled?

    (b) Payroll, tax, social security records?

    (c) Other records and reports-informing?

    (d) Departmental and general budgets?

(10) Public relations.

    (a) Haphazard, or planned?

    (b) who is responsible for a program?

    (c) Program adequate, up-to-date?

4. *Determining business objectives.* It has been well said that there is nothing about a business more important than its future. Where a company is going is more important than where it has been. The company that is satisfied to live on its past is headed down the hill; more alert competitors will soon overtake and pass it. That is why no business can afford to stand still; it must always be moving into the future.

But moving into the future should not be an operation in the dark. That is where objectives and goals prove their worth, serving as beacons and guides and enabling the business to move forward a step at a time. A newly organized company will have much planning to do-choosing what to sell, to whom, and in what territories. But companies of long standing, or of any age, need to take stock from time to time of where they are headed. The objectives that have guided them for a year, or five years, or even twenty years, may require revision in the light of changing markets or shifting economic conditions. Entirely new objectives may need to be added to their current goals.

Certain general objectives may be assumed for all companies, regardless of age or type. Thus, every concern wants to make a profit, keep out of debt as far as possible, obtain public good will, and so on. To be sure, these objectives may be held too vaguely to have much motivating effect on the business team, and may need pointing up to inspire more earnest effort, or to counteract a certain degree of negligence concerning them. To assume an objective without doing anything definite to realize it is an abuse of the term. An objective is something to work toward, with the accent on work. Anything less is merely pious wishing or daydreaming.

5. *Objectives motivate as well as direct.* Companies vary not only as to actual objectives but in the way they phrase their objectives. To stimulate a maximum of effort, an objective should be expressed in as specific a manner as possible-perhaps summed up, for everyday use, in a good slogan. The whole business team, working as well as executives, rallies enthusiasm, to an attractive slogan.

This was notably true during World War II, when catchy slogans on factory bulletin boards summarized the objective guiding the war production program. Typical of the others were these slogans: "America's Answer: Production"; "Give 'Em the Stuff to Fight With"; "Men working together"; "Idle Hands Work for Hitler." The objectives behind the slogans were important-overwhelming the enemy through sheer weight of munitions, securing maximum cooperation of workers, reducing absenteeism from factory and office tasks, raising the rate of war production in the shortest possible time. The workers sensed these objectives even as they rallied to the more colorful slogans that epitomized them.

Less dramatic, to be sure, are the objectives of peacetime production and distribution, yet they are far from being devoid of drama. Moreover, peacetime objectives can be translated into just as colorful slogans, as every sales contest or prize contest attests. In truth, the objectives of any going, progressive concern are a varied lot, capable of being summarized in terms of workers' personal interests, and so attaining their maximum motivating power.

Consider even a partial list of business objectives as reported by company executives during the past year:

(1) Widening the company's circle of customers.

(2) Developing new uses for an established product.

(3) Finding uses for by-products previously utilized.

(4) Attracting a higher type of employee.

(5) Concentrating sales effort on profitable outlets and weeding out unprofitable ones.

(6) Correcting public misunderstanding about company aims, profits, products or services.

(7) Winning acceptance for a new or improved product.

(8) Decentralizing production plants or warehouses, the better to serve distant markets.

(9) Improving relations with workers and labor unions, to secure better morale and cooperation.

(10) Freeing the company of debts or burdensome real-estate holdings tying up needed capital.

Any of the foregoing objectives could be used, as indeed they have been used, to give definite direction and guidance to a going business, while stimulating the fullest efforts of officers and workers to achieve the new goals thus set up.

6. *Formulation of master plans.* Business objectives involve the cooperation of many or all departments of the company. Each individual department assumes its part in carrying out the over-all objectives. To the end, it is a good practice to formulate a "master plan" for the department's activities, perhaps annually. Each such plan serves as a road map for that department's progress during the six months or twelve months that the plan is in effect. The plan directs the department's activities positively instead of leaving important matters, which should have been planned against in the beginning, to be handled by hit-or-miss methods or snap judgements as the problems appear.

Master plans are set up by conferences among the top executives of a business, or, in very important matters, by the board of directors. Department heads should be freely consulted during the formulation of a plan, since these are the men who will be expected to carry plans to a successful conclusion.

Examples of master plans usually set up on an annual basis are the following:

For Production: Lines to be produced, quantities to be made, periods when different items will be manufactured, new equipment to be bought.

For Marketing: Sales drives, lines to push, sales quotas, opening new markets.

For Advertising: Amounts to be spent, fields to be covered, periods of campaigns, media to be used.

For Finance: Estimates of income and expenditures, periods for borrowing, providing for special outlays, budgetary control devices.

7. *How management analyzes its problems.* Before a master plan can be formulated, or a major objective established, the management of a business must do a great deal of preliminary investigation-perhaps solve a whole series of problems or get the answers to numerous detailed questions. A new objective, or a new master plan, presupposes the determination of needs. Obstacles, economic conditions, markets, production costs, and so on, often in bewildering array.

The first step in the solution of any problem is to state the problem clearly. When it is thus specifically defined, it can usually be broken down into its elements. One by one, these elements may then be studied until the point offers the real difficulty is discovered. With the investigation thus narrowed down to one specific factor, either past experience, some other company's action under similar conditions, consulting advice, or research may bring to light the possible means of solution.

It may be necessary to investigate several possible alternatives rather carefully, or try one or more of them experimentally before the right solution is discovered. But no problem is ever solved as a whole. It must be broken down into its parts, and each subproblem tackled in its turn.

For example, the problem may be proposed to introduce a new food product on the market. The elements of this problem are:

Will it have any special appeal to prospective buyers?

What is the nature of the appeal?

Will it find most favor with men, with housewives or with children?

Will it be in a price class or for the general markets?

Are there any special regions or any particular kinds of people to whom it will most appeal?

How wide a market will it be profitable to attempt to reach?

Should it be introduced gradually, community by community, or at once on a national scale?

At what price should it sell to reach an economic point of distribution?

Can it be produced and marketed to bring in a profit at this price?

How much investment in equipment, sales promotion, etc., will be required to get the product on the market?

Can the money be provided for this purpose?

How long a time will elapse before the product probably will return the cost of putting it on the market?

What are competitors producing, or what are they likely to produce, of a similar kind?

These are only a few of the questions that might be involved, but they are all elements of the main problem. The answer to the question, "Shall we put out this product?" is not decided by saying right off, "Yes, it will be a money-maker," or "No, we will lose on out." Many of the elements may be highly favorable for going ahead, but some factors may be a vital point on which the final answer is definitely determined.

8. *Growth of management with growth of the business.* A primary task in business management is the creation of a reliable, hard-hitting organization. Management is a many-sided job, regardless of the size of the business, but, in the beginning, the operating organization may be small. One or two men, at first-partners in a business newly born-may constitute the management, concentrating in their own hands all the functions of the many departments and sub-departments of a large company. Much must necessarily be neglected or ignored that the large business would undertake to perform, but none of its really essential functions.

Just as a large company must do, the partners of a newly launched business must decide what they will produce or purchase for resale, raise the capital needed for getting the business started, find a good location, secure equipment and materials, hire workmen or salesmen or clerks, induce customers to buy their product or goods or service, decide who may have credit and discounts, press collections if necessary, and set up some kind of accounting and cost control.

Other managerial functions are involved in the minimum schedule of our imaginary partners, who are doubtless the supreme example of business executives with a many-sided job. If their business prospers and expands, the partners will need executive assistance, over and above the working and clerical personnel. In time, regular departments will be set up to take over the more pressing functions, such as accounting, purchasing, production or sales. There may be a legal reorganization to get more working capital, which incorporation may more easily provide. The partners will doubtless become the top officers of the new corporation, but they will share executive responsibility with a board of directors. Expanding business will result in an expansion of management-perhaps also in an expansion of ownership vested in a growing family of stockholders.

Every step in this expansion brings with it new problems-legal, economic, financial, and operating. To solve these problems, management will need to call upon various kinds of experts for advice-lawyers, economists, research men, advertising agencies, traffic managers, insurance and real estate men, etc. In some cases, it will pay to add such experts to the management staff; in others, to retain or consult them only for specific problems as needed. But in the long run, everything will depend upon the quality of the regular management itself. If the officers and department heads have the ability to face their real problems, and to analyze them correctly, the business will reach its goals.

9. *Setting up management controls.* Once the problems of what to do and how to do it are solved, the next step is to push "full-steam" ahead. It is then that the matter of controls becomes especially vital. The business team must pull together, in the same direction, at the same rate, with perfect timing. Management must assume the job of the coxswain who directs the pace and inspires perfect coordination.

Does every department understand its part in the over-all objective? Are any unforeseen obstacles, material or human, arising to snag the department's progress, thereby holding back the progress of other departments? Some system of communications and controls must be devised to answer and meet these questions.

In general, there are five broad lines of communication at the service of the management-lines of control which are also sources of information about the progress of business. These information and control devices are:

(1) Personal observation, involving tours of inspection.

(2) Interviews and conferences with department heads.

(3) Financial statements and budgetary reports.

(5) Special or research reports, from either committees or qualified individuals.

First-hand observation is the simplest and, in some ways, the best control device-at least there is no adequate substitute for it. Face-to-face contacts with the men who are doing the job not only give the best opportunity for ironing out misunderstandings, but also for renewing workers' morale. There is not much inspiration for workers under a regime of strictly "swivel-chair management," and the executive who holds to his office as to an ivory tower is taking the one sure method of losing touch with his business.

Interviews and conferences with departmental heads, or with foremen and workers, may be occasional for some, regular for others. In either case, such conferences will seem more realistic to those who are making oral reports to management if the top executive has acquired a fund of up-to-date information about the company operations through personal observation. It is true, of course, that the executive's time is limited, that necessary correspondence and conferences often prevent the following of a regular schedule of personal visits. Oral reports by department heads, either individually or in a group conference, make up for unavoidable postponement of inspection tours, and give a more complete picture of current operations and problems.

The pressure of business is often so intense, and the executive's time so limited, that neither of these two devices will suffice, even when they can be scheduled. Moreover, the results of interviews and personal tours are not usually available in writing, for future comparison and study. It is to supply this lack that management has recourse to a carefully selected series of departmental reports, submitted on a schedule.

10. *Control through reports*. Reports have further advantage of freeing the management from unnecessary detail. They present only the essential facts needed for arriving at a decision. In an interview or conference, some time is almost sure to be wasted in discussing unnecessary details or some point irrelevant to the purpose of the conference. Reports go straight to the point irrelevant to the purpose of the conference. Reports go straight to the point, particularly those reports submitted on standard forms. Moreover, unpleasant as well as pleasant facts about the business appear as a matter of course on report forms-facts that an employee might not have the courage to present orally, knowing as he does, that bad news invites a reprimand.

Accounting and cost reports are especially impersonal, giving management the cold facts as to production, sales, collections, inventories, labor costs and literally dozens of other pertinent kinds of data. It is true, of course, that a well designed form will give more information than a poorly designed one. Because forms can confuse and obscure rather than clarify, form design is a technique worthy of careful study.

Over the years, the accounting profession has done much to improve the collection of vital business data and their presentation in forms most useful to management. Accounting reports are in a true sense the progress charts for the business, showing the actual trend of affairs, and especially whether the business is realizing its paramount objective-the making of profits. The obstacles to profit-making are also clearly indicated in a good accounting report.

Reports at stated intervals on how closely each department is living up to its master plan or budget are likewise important for the detection of obstacles to profit-making. Making a budget is good; better still is the submission of performance figures showing how closely the budget has been adhered to. It is the checking of performance against plans and estimates that establishes budgetary *control*, as distinct from budget-making or planning.

11. *The dangers of prosperity*. Management controls operate most easily in a period of tense struggle, when business is slow or when the company is engaged in an all-out effort to win success. In such a period, management is alert to every market opportunity, and watchful of every item of expense tending to absorb more than its rightful share of the company's capital. No detail of management is overlooked.

Let success and prosperity come, with sales running high and orders pouring in, and management tends to relax. It is then that each department discovers how many new tools and gadgets it could use, or how much more it could accomplish if its personnel were doubled.

If top management settles into an expansive mood, nodding approval of each departmental request, it may soon find itself in the fanned state of "profitless prosperity"-that is, income will be high but profits will be proportionately lower, and perhaps actually lower. Operating costs will have eaten up the increased income. To make matters worse, it is very hard to shift back to a less costly operating level.

It is not merely a matter of curbing the impulse to spend, important as that may be. Management must go farther, must determine well as it can the causes of success, and the conditions that allow these causes to operate favorably. It may be that expansion and spending are in order; that now, or never, the company must decide how large it wants to be, and take the steps necessary to attain or maintain it optimum size. In that event, profits may have to be plowed back into the business for a more or less indefinite period. This spending should not be wasteful, however.

12. *The human problems of management*. The production man tends to think of his work in terms of materials, machines, and assembly lines. The sales manager may become engrossed, at least temporarily, in market statistics, sales potentials and sales quotas. The comptroller sees the business as a moving graph of up and down curves, standing for changing assets and liabilities. These various economic entities almost assume a life of their own, as if endowed with personality. Business planning, aiming at ever greater efficiency, comes to resemble

equations and formulas of the mathematician. But these
viewpoints are illusions.

The realities of business are people-the people who buy or
may buy the product or service, the workers and managers, their
families and dependents, the suppliers of raw materials and
tools, all of whom directly or indirectly are affected by the
operations of the business. Machines, assembly lines, sales
promotions and financial statements do exist to serve them-must
not be permitted to eclipse them, or to obscure their needs as
persons. The rapidity with which science has showered new tools
upon business has tended to make human engineering lag behind
the engineering of materials. The task of management is now
seen to be that of closing this gap-of giving the human factor
the attention that it deserves. That is why industrial and
public relations are being studied and promoted with new
earnestness by modern management.

Advisory 4

The Executive Image

1. *Three classes of men.* Plato divide the people of his ideal republic into three classes: the philosophers, who were to do the thinking and ruling; their lieutenants, who were to execute orders; and the great mass of the people, who were to continue, most of them, to be slaves.

The French Montesquieu, of a much later century, also divided mankind into three classes: first, those who are able to think, to give the world new ideas; second, men who cannot do original thinking but who can understand the ideas of the first class; third, men who apparently do not wish to think or try to understand the thinking done by others.

The German Nietzsche, in the nineteenth century, drew up a still harsher classification. The topmost group he dubbed supermen. They were superior to the masses of men and could not be held subject to the laws made for the common people; the superman obeyed only the laws which he himself made. Nietzsche's second class of men consisted of those intelligent enough to understand and execute the will of the supermen. The "common herd" comprised his third class, of no social consequence.

If we were to accept these views, implying the existence of insurmountable walls between different classes of men, so that a man born into one class could never climb into the one above, we should rightfully think this is a very sorry world indeed. Under such circumstances, the work of all educational institutions would lose its most compelling motive-the development of men's latent powers in order that they may rise to higher levels and lead more efficient lives. But we know that man is not like a tree or an animal; by his own will he can escape from a narrow environment, and by his own will he can loosen the fetters which he may have inherited from a backward ancestry.

Nevertheless, men do differ widely in their characteristics. We all know men who are natural leaders, men whom others instinctively trust and follow; also men who man excellent lieutenants or assistants, but who need the guidance of leaders in order to rise to higher responsibilities; also the millions who have not advanced to positions where they do important planning or directing. Of this latter group, a large portion are leading constructive lives in occupations which nowadays demand a grade of thinking far superior to that of former days in the same callings. But there are still multitudes of people who prefer to be led, and who seem to be content to continue performing only such tasks as they have mastered through imitation and practice, finding a form of security in the routine with which their lives are filled.

The man who is *content* with routine work is not likely to be reading this book; he is satisfied with the security he has, it is not aspiring to an executive position. It is the man spurred on by "divine discontent" who investigates what he must do to rise above his present economic level and to win the opportunity of engaging in more interesting and rewarding activities.

Such a man knows that his advancement depends upon himself, that no power on earth can take a clerk from his desk or a mechanic from his bench and mold him into an executive, as by a miracle. Self-advancement is powered by one's own initiative and perseverance; the help of others is secondary. Their help may be very useful, but is still secondary.

2. *What is an executive*? In a word, he is a business leader, a man who (in the phrasing of the dictionary) is "active, skillful or especially fitted for directing the

enforcement of judgements or the conduct of affairs." To some degree, varying according to whether a man is a top, an intermediate, or a junior executive, the business leader organizes and directs, makes decisions and give orders. He may receive some orders, also, and may have had only a small hand in framing them, or none at all. Nevertheless, he is entrusted with the enforcement of the policies formulated by higher executives or by a board of directors. His is the task of coordinating men and materials, tools and finances, creating order and unified effort. Like the quarterback on a football team, he calls the signals.

The executive tasks of coordination and direction are carried forward on every level of the business, in every division, department and subdepartment. The opportunities for executive activity vary from large to small, are often mixed with activities which plainly are not directive at all, but operational. Thus, the head of the sales department may try his hand at selling an usually important customer or prospect and when he is so engaged, he is acting as a salesman rather than a sales executive.

Again, some men are classed as executives who are really advisers to executives. They do not give orders to the rank and file of workers, to factory foremen or salesmen or store buyers. They conduct investigations of market conditions, or purchase supplies, or plan and place the company's advertising. They advise the management in charge of workmen or salesmen about economic trends, or about special difficulties and how to surmount them, or about new opportunities for products or sales. They are the staff officers in the business army-not the line officers-yet custom classes them as executives along with the others, and rightly so, since they are helping to draft policies.

Clearly, then, "business executive" is an omnibus term, including men holding a great variety of directive and advisory positions and differing degrees of responsibility for results. The executive group ranges from a board of directors at the top (in a corporation) and the company officers, down through a fairly long line of intermediate and junior executives to the level of supervisors and foremen, where executive and routine duties become difficult to distinguish.

3. *Four levels of management*. The executive group has grown rapidly during the past few decades, to keep pace with the

growth of operating and advisory departments. The expansion of industrial and marketing research, the building and maintenance of larger plants, the growth of new techniques in sales promotion, purchasing, accounting and in industrial and public relations, have created an almost bewildering array of new departments, each with its own executives.

Not only are there many new positions in executive organizations, but there are also new titles for some of the older positions. Thus, the employment manager of earlier years has become the personnel manager of today. Again, executive titles vary widely from company to company, often overlapping and obscuring the degree of responsibility behind each title. Some variations are local, others regional.

Allowing for these difficulties, it is possible to establish certain broad levels of management, based on the functions or services of each to the company. Four such levels may be indicated, as follows:

(1) The board of directors.

(2) Company officers-top management.

(3) Divisional executives-intermediate management.

(4) Departmental executives-junior management.

A fifth level might be composed of the assistants, supervisors and foremen whose duties are partly executive and partly routine.

4. *Functions on the management levels*. The board of directors (the first management level) exercises a trusteeship function, representing and safeguarding the interests of the stockholders, protecting and insuring the most effective use of the company's assets, approving the over-all policies of the business, and reviewing the results of company operations.

The top management, in the hands of the company officers, has charge of the planning and control of the business as a whole, within the limits of policy and authority established by the board of directors. Top management decides upon the company's day-to-day objectives and policies, and checks the results.

Intermediate management, represented in some companies by the heads of divisions, and in others by various staff and operating committees, has charge of broad segments of the business and is responsible to the company officers. The divisions may be based on geography, with a division for each region of the country and another for overseas trade.

In other companies, divisions may be based on product lines, as, for example, a company that maintains a radio division, a second division for electronic devices, a third for television equipment, and so on. Still another example of intermediate management is the assignment of broad functions to general committees, as, for example, a committee on products, another on personnel, a third on public relations, etc.

Within the various divisions of a company, or working under general committees, are the departments set up to carry out specialized objectives. In many companies, perhaps a majority, the departments dominate the operating organization, and no groupings into divisions are provided for. In that case, department heads are intermediate or even major executives. Moreover, custom assigns a greater importance of the department is a determining factor.

One practice is shared in common: the title of junior executive is likely to be applied to all those who assist a department or division heads in more than a merely clerical capacity. Helping the department head plan his work, acting in his place when he is absent or busy with other affairs, serving as his representative or "trouble-shooter" with some authority to get action, the junior executive is an active and trusted lieutenant, destined, in the normal course of events, for increased responsibilities and a higher position. His future is mainly in his own hands.

5. *The work of the top executive*. Ideally, the top executives are set free from the routine detail of lesser executives in order that they may concentrate on the larger problems of the business. Practically, this ideal of freedom from routine is imperfectly realized-sometimes, we shall see, through the executive's own fault. There are other obstacles of course; one being the inability of management to agree on what the major problems of a business really are. The previous experience of an executive sometimes clouds his judgment as to what is major and what is minor.

The man who becomes a top executive after years of service as a salesman and assistant sales manager will be inclined to put marketing problems ahead of all others. The executive who reaches the top via the factory or mill will tend to stress production and supply problems. The man who has specialized in the financial problems of business will emphasize the factors of risk and cost involved in every new project.

In general, however, top executives will agree on at least a minimum list of tasks that should take precedence of othrs. They will agree, for example, that it is their duty to watch closely the reports from department heads showing the progress, or lack of progress, of the business. As long as these reports correspond to the master plans approved for the year, or with departmental budgets, it is evident that everything is going well. If, on the contrary, the reports show some unusual departure from the plan or budget-some sign of financial imbalance, perhaps-the top executives will call for an immediate explanation or investigation. It may be only temporary difficulty, easily overcome; then, again, the obstacle to progress may be a serious one, requiring a revamping of master plans.

6.*Studying economic and social trends*. A second concern of the top executive, by general assent, is that of studying economic and social trends likely to affect his particular business. Among possible economic trends may be the approach of inflation of deflation, industrial concentration or decentralization, shifting populations affecting established markets, an increase of buying power among hitherto low-income groups, consumer resistance to prices and styles, and so on.

Social trends may include changes in consumers' living conditions and wants, an increase in the birth rate, a change in the proportion of women or of older people in a given population, the effects of migration and immigration, and the like. Any of these trends may signal the approaching end of some company activity or the opening up of new opportunities. The top executive is the man who must appraise the meaning of each signal for his company and decide what to do about it.

Social trends may include attitudes as well as physical or biological changes. The attitudes of people toward a particular company, toward some department of business (advertising, for example, or toward business in general, may help or hinder successful operations. If popular attitudes are consistently unfavorable, it may be that a job in public relations work is in order. Perhaps the key to the difficulty lies in a better handling of industrial relations. Perhaps, again, the task of correcting negative attitudes is one that requires the cooperation of an entire industry, working through its trade association.

Sometimes a popular misapprehension is played up to the point where it is embodied in state or federal legislation. Laws regulating business do not always originate in a popular prejudice, of course; on the contrary, a regulatory law may be necessary to correct an abuse which business has not been able or willing to correct. In either case, it is the top executive, assisted by legal counsel, who must appraise the difference that an actual or proposed law may make in company operations. Membership in an alert trade association is a great help in making due allowance for the effects of proposed or actual legislation.

7. *Building a good organization*. There is also a general agreement that a major task of the top executive is the creation of a loyal and efficient organizations. A business is as good as the men behind it, and no better. If good men are to be retained, however, they must be placed in the right positions for making full use of their social talents and given as much responsibility and authority as each position requires for turning in a good performance. Every executive should have the opportunity of growing on his job, of taking on greater tasks as he becomes ready for them.

The building of an executive organization is so important that it ought never to be undertaken by a man who has not himself been well trained in business. A man without experience, no matter how much capital he possesses, should beware of making the experiment. To such a man, business may seem a simple matter, just as a baseball looks like a very easy game to the inexperienced spectator. The better the players, the easier the game looks. So for business-the more experienced it executives, the more smoothly a company's operations go forward. But the job of assembling and coordinating a really efficient business organization requires considerably more knowledge and judgement than the building of a championship baseball team.

The most fundamental consideration in setting up any organization is first to determine the specific function to be carried on. The men to carry out these functions can be selected later. It may not be possible, at first, to get the idea man for every function; some shuffling and reshuffling may be necessary until every man is put in the position where he can best utilize his knowledge and abilities.

Fitting the man to the job is important, but it will not do to build an executive organization around a handful of brilliant men, regardless of the functional needs of the business. Such a procedure leads to waste and duplication, for it may easily happen (often has, in fact) that the men for whom jobs must be found are too similar in training and ability. The business really needs one president, but not two; one comptroller, one advertising manager, one factory superintendent, one head buyer, and so on. If there are two ideal candidates for a specific job among the available executives, one man is going to be placed happily, and the other where he will be either a misfit or an unhappy mediocrity.

Another danger must be considered. If an organization is built up around men instead of around functions, and those men fail, or leave, or die, the whole organizational structure may be weakened ot may topple. Even though things do not go that far, an organization built around men almost invariably develops departmental jealousies and faulty morale. Since the jobs have been set up to make use of available men, functions cannot be too sharply defined or delimited, and the inevitable result is confusion, "sniping," and jealousy. If the business goes ahead, it is in spite of its organization pattern, rather than because of it. One or two brilliant leaders may carry the team along with them through the sheer force of their initiative and daring, but if anything happens to stop them or to cause them to drop out entirely, the organization flounders badly through want of any clear-cut definition of its duties.

8. *Delegating responsibilities*. When the objectives and functions of a business have been carefully explained and put in charge of the best men available, the next step is to give this executive organization full trust and responsibility. For some top executives, this is a hard step to take. The founder of a business, in particular, is prone to feel that nothing will be rightly done unless he does it himself, or at least has finger in the pie. To hold to such an attitude is, of course, to show that he does not understand the principles of executive organization, or cannot rise to the type of leadership demanded in a growing business.

The leaders of a growing business, having selected their lieutenants because of their training and ability, should leave to them the actual management of departmental activities. Assuming that the division and department heads have been given clear and definite descriptions of their duties, they should also be given full authority and responsibility to carry these duties out. It is for the top executives to coordinate and correlate the activities of the various divisions so that the major politics and plans of the company are achieved.

In doing so, the top executive should not dictate or meddle in the details of divisional work, so long as this work is being carried out according to plan. Regular reports and conferences will establish the facts about the company's progress. Where a company runs into difficulties proceeding from poor teamwork or executive morale. The root of the trouble is often to be found in the tendency of some top executive to interfere with divisional or departmental operations.

The interfering executive may have come up through one of the divisions from whose activities he can never quite divorce himself. He is always fussing over the work of this division, and attempting to steer its operation. Instead of letting the new division manager apply his own ideas and perhaps make some worthwhile improvements in methods and results, the president becomes nervous when plans he formerly followed are changed or abandoned. To him, such a departure just cannot be right, so he steps in and practically directs that things be done as he used to do them. Then the division manager gives up and stops trying to develop his division. It is better, he thinks, to be a "yes" man and hold his job, or at least avoid arguments, than to keep on with improvements that would be of profit to the company.

The story is told that Andrew Carnegie, while going through one of his big steel mills with its manager, Captain Bill Jones, a famous steelmaster, and directing that many things be done, remarked, "You don't know haw glad I'll be this time next week." "Why?" asked Captain Jones. "I'll be on my way back to Scotland for a rest," was Mr. Carnegie's reply. "well," said Captain Jones, who had known his employer for many years, "you can't tell how glad we'll be, too."

9. *The Principle of Exceptions*. To be most successful, a chief executive must reserve his special talents and energies for the things which give the most serious trouble and are important enough to require official decision or action. Most

of the problems down the line within a division can be adequately settled by the division manager. The division manager will never learn to do his best if he does not find out how to solve difficulties, unsnarl tangles, and direct his workers efficiently. Moreover, if his decisions are always made for him by his chief, he will have no confidence in his own ability. Many a business man has blamed his division heads for lapses and failures when he himself has undermined their authority, confidence and ability by taking over their worries and trying to solve their problems. The most efficient assistants are those whom the head of the company has learned to let make mistakes so that the next time they will know better and definitely do the right thing.

By thus conserving his efforts to handle the big problems and the unusual variations from the plans laid out for operation, the top executive has the time and energy to direct the larger affairs of his company and accomplish its aims. He can devote his attention to exceptions from the usual routine. This principle is very important in any line of business activity.

Through regular reports from his divisional heads, the chief executive keeps informed on the progress of work or developments in each division. As long as these reports check with the master plans previously laid out for the year, month or other period of operation, then it is evident that everything is going along as scheduled, and the executive need have no worries. But if the reports indicate abnormal variations from the plan, he can at once investigate and take whatever action is necessary.

One president has presented to him, monthly, summarized cost reports showing for each successive month the average unit cost on each line of equipment manufactured in his plant. If these costs check within a small percentage with "standard cost" figures for each line, he knows that operations in this respect have been carried on successfully. If there are variations, say, of more than two or three per cent, then he has the opportunity of making an investigation, while his department heads and foremen have the facts in mind, to find out the cause of variation. If it was unpreventable and will persist, he can change the "standards" against which he checks. If inefficiencies have brought about the troubles, he can act to have the causes removed. If some saving has been found possible, he can make it a permanent reduction in material or operating cost.

Another president was able comfortably to take a long vacation in Florida because he had developed with his assistants a series of "ratios" of operation which gave him the key as to when various important factors in his business were all right, and provided danger signals when operations were not progressing properly. His staff sent him periodic statements as to the current ratios at the time of each report, and, since there was never any variation which could not be corrected without his return to his business, he was able to secure a rest free from worries as to how things were going while he was away.

The Principle of Exceptions applies equally well to the work of other executives, division managers, and, in fact, to the activities of all those in supervisory positions. Its proper understanding and application should be encouraged by the head of the enterprise so that the best energies f the entire staff can be freed from unnecessary routine checks and inspections and concentrated in the new problems arising to give special and often serious trouble.

10. *The executive as a pioneer.* Running a business by means of cost reports and operating ratios is possible, obviously, only when the business is well established or when no major change of direction is at hand. But there are times for every business (always, of course, when it is getting started, but also possible later in its history) when new plans must be tries and extensive experiments conducted. It is at such times that the executive has the opportunity of becoming a business pioneer, assuming that he has within him the requisite resourcefulness and daring. If he runs at all true to type, he will not be found lacking.

Typically, the business man has always been a pioneer, undertaking undreamed-of projects. He is the man who combined a few small railways into great transportation systems, who organized bus and motortrucking lines spanning the continent, who is today pioneering in passenger and freight transportation by air. In the field of production, he discovered the opportunities for lower costs and wider distribution latent in mass production, and to that end developed the integrated manufacturing plant and the huge assembly line.

It was the business pioneer, also, who saw the possibilities inherent in the postal service and so created great mail-order businesses. Envisioning mass distribution, he brought into being the department store, the retail chain, and the supermarket. Wherever he discovered wastes in old-fashioned procedures, obsolescence in equipment, decadence in thinking and planning, he struck out boldly along new and untried lines to change the face of the business world.

Deeds like these we have mentioned are accomplished only by the greatest executives-men who combine to a high degree the qualities of the dreamer and the practical builder. Their gifts of constructive imagination are beyond the average, yet what they have and do is reproduced on a smaller scale all down the line in the business world. Constructive imagination and administrative leadership are no monopoly of the few; on the contrary, they are shared in some measures by every executive who succeeds in doing more than break even. On every level, the work of business creation goes forward. The ability to originate is typical of the successful executive.

11. *What else must the executive be?* The executive must do more than originate. He must be able not merely to plan but also to push plans through to successful execution. He must be able, therefore, to direct others how to carry out his purposes. He must pick men who will understand his objectives and he must see that his instructions are obeyed. In sum, the top executives of an enterprise need all the qualities characterizing a man of action and accomplishment, plus the intellectual power to study and plan. The larger the business, the greater are the responsibilities of its officers, and the greater, also, are their opportunities.

On the intellectual side, the top executive has need of an orderly and "scientific" type of mind. At the same time, he should possess a vivid, constructive imagination, and intuitive knowledge of men, and a personality which makes others rally to him as a leader. He should preferably radiate energy and enthusiasm. He must have sound judgement, keen discernment, the power of prompt decision, and a willingness to accept and discharge heavy possibilities. His power to coordinate varied activities should be above average.

Toward his executive staff, his assistants and his employees he must be just, consistent, kindly, cheerful and able to exercise self-control. He must believe in others, be receptive to suggestions, take an active interest in the progress of his executives and employees, listen impartially to grievances brought to his attention, settle differences fairly, and keep his door open to anyone in the company who has a problem yo solve which cannot be answered satisfactorily anywhere down the line. Through such qualities he can instill a spirit of unbeatable teamwork throughout his entire organization and inspire his associates, individually and collectively, with the will to achieve.

12. *Great leasers are courageous*. The executive who believes in his company will have positive convictions as to its worthiness and the necessity for discharging his responsibilities to the best interest of his organization. His convictions will form the basis for courage in carrying them out. If he feels that a certain step is right he will take it even though a great effort may be required to put it in effect. A moral coward, one who is afraid to do what he thinks is right because other men will disapprove, is never a confident business man not a valuable member of any community. In business, cowardice of any kind is a serious detriment, for it will make a man hesitate and hang back at the very moment he should be forging full-steam ahead.

The business executive must be resolute and stout of heart. He must not fear his competitors, but must meet their rivalry with the spirit of refusing to be defeated. If he is opposed in his own organization, he must meet the issue squarely. Should he prove to be wrong, he should frankly admit his mistake. If he has every reason to believe he is right, he should hold his ground firmly but without rancor.

All great business men have been courageous. They have dared things which would have frightened and paralyzed weaker men. The odds were often against them, but they kept on fighting. They had courage as well as initiative.

The Up & Coming Junior Executive

1. *Who are junior executives*? A man entitled to be regarded as a junior executive when his duties in the organization require the exercise of independent judgement and discretion in the handling of business responsibilities. If he

has charge of merely of the routine work of a group of men, his principle duty being to see that their work is done on time and in the proper manner, he may be a supervisor or head clerk, but he does not rank as a junior executive. To reach that level, he must have the authority to wrestle directly with business problems as they occur-to analyze them, to make plans, to initiate action. Some problems, involving factors outside his own department, he will refer to the senior or top executives for solution, or perhaps for their approval of his solution.

The business problems confronting a junior executive may not appear very difficult in comparison with the complex production or financial problems that frequently beset the top executive. Very often, they are not. On the other hand, it would be a mistake to underestimate the junior executive's task. His problems appear simpler mainly because they crop up in smaller segment of the business-a department, a subdepartment, or a section. The abilities required to solve the problems of the department are important; essentially, they are much the same as those demanded of the top executive. If they were not, the junior executive would not receive the training enabling him, when the opportune moment arrives, to move up to the senior level and to take over the work of some intermediate or top executive who has retired or moved on.

It is rightly said that a chain is as strong as its weakest link. If that link breaks, the entire chain is put out of commission. No part of a business, therefore, is unimportant; each has its necessary part in the sum total of activities by means of which business achieves its objectives and earns its profits. By that token, the work of the junior executive must be taken for what it really is, a serious contribution to business success. Its efficient performance is a matter of concern to every member of the organization, from the president down. So, too, are the recruitment, the training and the care of the junior executive.; Much, if not most, of the top management of the business in future years will be drawn from the ranks of its junior executives. Their effectiveness on the top level of management will depend directly upon the opportunities that have been given them to develop their executive talents during the years while they were heads and assistant heads of departments. Those opportunities should be made as abundant as possible.

2. *Duties and responsibilities*. The first duty of a junior executive is to make himself as useful as possible to top management. He is a lieutenant, holding delegated powers and taking care of matters that once, when the company was in its infancy, were the concern of the senior executives. He must try to catch the viewpoint of top management, and see beyond the confines of his own particular department, so as to gain an overview of how his work fits into the general pattern of company activities. Unless he can take this broader view of his job, he will not qualify for advancement into the ranks of wither intermediate or top management, no matter what may be his other talents.

Besides looking up, the junior executive must look down. He should be alert to discover men who can be trained for leadership. Such men, when found, should be qualified as understudies for every executive position in his department, including his own. If the business executive takes seriously this talk of discovering and training executive talent, the business will never lack for administrative ability. Sudden death or an unexpected resignation will not cause the organization to falter or perhaps stumble and go down.

Within his department, the junior executive will set up procedures and controls based on the objectives and policies determined by top management or by the board of directors. He will strive for a smooth-running, efficient department, imbued with high morale and the realization that all are working to provided a product or service of genuine worth to the community and the nation.

The junior executive will realize that he is a detail man *par excellence*. Together with the other junior executives, he is taking over the run-of-the-mill problems so that top management may be as free as possible to concentrate on the larger administrative and planning tasks. Top management sets the objectives, but it is intermediate and junior management which must carry the lion's share of the detailed activities.

3. *Qualifications and training*. Physically, the junior executive should have an ample fund of constitutional vigor to sustain him in his difficult duties. Leadership makes heavy demands upon energy and stamina. The listless, languid man will hardly amount to much as an executive, but he should not be confused with the man whose health is known to be only moderately good. The latter may support his mediocre health by

careful habits of living, and thus obtain a sufficient physical background for executive work.

What we call energy in a man is the product of physical vigor, or health, and of a purpose, or end, clearly conceived and strongly desired. An energetic man thinks quickly, feels strongly, and acts decisively. But the energy which the executive needs should not be confused with its counterfeit-a pretentious, bustling kind of activity concerned with petty affairs. The really energetic man is usually not a spendthrift, either with words or deeds. He wants every act to count, to be worth doing.

On the intellectual side, the junior executive should have one ability to a degree better than the average, namely, the ability to single out essential factors in a situation and to see how they are related to one another. This power of analysis should be united to a temperamental ability to reach conclusions and make decisions. The business man must think rapidly, and rarely has time to ponder over a problem for the sheer delight in speculating about it. That is not to say that he should encourage himself to become hasty or superficial, but merely that he cannot delay a decision for the sake of exploring its theoretical aspects, as a researcher, a judge or a philosopher might do. Thinking of that type is a luxury the executive cannot usually afford.

A college education is usually as asset to the junior executive, although that depends on what he got out of it and his conception of how to use it. In general, it should have taught him how to think, imbuing his mental powers with a certain flexibility often lacking in persons of less education. General culture and a well rounded education assist the young executive in his contacts with superiors and with men outside his company, but general information and good manners are possessions which the self-made man can also acquire if he is willing to make an effort.

The young executive must possess a general knowledge of the business or industry into which he enters, plus a detailed knowledge of the work of his own department. Any position to which he is assigned may include the supervision of some section of the business not covered by his previous experience. He may be unfamiliar with some of its special techniques, but this will not matter so long as he can grasp the broad essentials of the work. The specialist must know the detailed techniques; the executive must be able to judge the efficiency with which the techniques are being applied, and whether the section is accomplishing its allotted share of the business task. As time goes on, the executive will also come to know much of the technique itself, but efficiency is his main concern.

The junior executive's knowledge of the business may be derived from years of experience workman, foreman, clerk or assistant. Sometimes he may come to his position from a university school of business administration, where he learned the general principles and much of the detail of conducting marketing or financial activities. In addition, he may have pursued a cooperative program, giving half of his time to college studies and the other half to actual experience in business. Or he may have taken most of his college work at night while holding down a job during the daytime hours.

The quality of such practical experience will determine whether his employers can start him as a junior executive or must require him to learn the business from the ground up. Where this process must be followed, it should be managed in a way to shorten the learner's time and to capitalize on his training.

4. *What the beginner wants from his employer*. A large group of engineering students enrolled in the course in Economics and Administration at Clarkson College were recently polled on what the college graduate has a right to expect from his first employer. Five points outranked all the others: (1) Tolerance and patience; (2) training and good supervision: (3) opportunities for advancement; (4) information at regular intervals on the beginner's progress; (5) recognition as a person. These are astonishingly thoughtful expectations.

Tomorrow's production man hopes that his first employer will be tolerant and patient. The beginner is bound to meet with many new and strange problems, some of which, being human, he will probably bungle. How will his superiors react to his mistake? If they will display understanding and patience, the beginner will not take as long to regain his self-confidence. As one student out it, "The young engineer should have a right to make a mistake, but he should not have the right to keep on making that mistake over and over again." Most business men would agree to that statement of the limits of tolerance.

The university or college graduate recognizes the limited scope and theoretical nature of his preparation and wants further training. "I do not expect my employer," wrote one student," to make my job a bed of roses, but I do expect a reasonable amount of help in my beginning at his plant." Other students said they would consider the element of supervision as one of the most important attractions of a prospective position. If there were a choice of companies, they would take the one offering the most supervision. Their idea, obviously, is to get maximum training.

The point about opportunities for advancement, according to the Clarkson students, is that they should be there "where you can see them." Promotions have to be earned and need not come rapidly, but the beginning executive wants to know that they will come when deserved.

Beginners are most anxious to know how they are doing. They would like to have progress reports of some sort at regular intervals, presumably through a discussion of the results that the beginner has been able to obtain. If the senior executives come to the conclusion that he beginner is out of his element and should make a change, the beginner would like to be told. And he would like to be told before it is too late to take up some other line of endeavor.

Finally, the novice executive would like his employer to recognize him as a person, to create the feeling that the two are working together in a common enterprise rather than carrying out a master-servant situation. The trained man is and should be proud of what he is and of what he stands for. "All he asks is a chance to prove himself.

5. *Developing leaders*. During his earlier years in business, a man's talents may remain more or less hidden. He does not know his own abilities or what his future may be. As long as he remains in a subordinate position below the executive level, he may do his work ever so conscientiously without giving any sign of the real power within him. When such a man is given a position carrying some responsibility, his latent quality comes to surface and is discovered. His advancement thereafter is limited only by only his mental and physical powers, assuming, of course, that he is connected with a growing business.

It takes responsibility to develop the power of leadership. No man knows his power over men until he has been tested, just as no man knows whether he is brave or not until he has been under fire. Ulysses S. Grant, a graduate of West Point who had served in the Mexican War, was a modest nobody when the Civil war broke out in 1861. But for that war, he probably would have lived and died in obscurity. The war developed in him the latent quality if leadership and he became one of the great generals of all time.

It is important that young men in business should not be kept forever at the same tasks, for their finest qualities may then never be brought out. Leadership is not developed by limiting the junior executive's field of action.

Unfortunately, not ever young man welcomes responsibility or is willing to assume the load that comes with it. Perhaps he does not realize that therein lies his one sure road to advancement, or perhaps he is constitutionally or temperamentally unfitted for executive work. If he really wants to advance, however, he will gladly take on all responsibilities that are offered him. He may be sure that they will not be offered to him faster than he is ready for them. The progressive-minded employer not only watches carefully over the development of his junior executives, but is continually looking for men who welcome responsibility.

6. *What may the employer expect*? We come now to the employer's expectations-what he hopes to find in the novice executive. In general, he expects what he demands of himself, only in less developed degree, allowing for the factors of youthfulness and inexperience. All executives, whether senior or junior, should possess considerable initiative, high integrity, positive dependability, and definite coordinative ability. Without these general qualities, no executive's success in business will be noteworthy.

These comprehensive abilities and qualities are not the whole story; there are others that the junior executive should have if he is to become what his employer expects him to be-a directive force in the business. In any event, the quality of his work will be reflected in the course of business. If the junior executive makes mistakes, the business will suffer loss. If he directs his department wisely, the profits and goodwill of the business will be increased.

Many lists have been drawn up from time to time in an effort to delineate the ideal executive. Regardless of their variations, they contain much of service to the junior executive, for whom they are primarily intended. He is setting up personal ideals to guide his future career. He is trying to form useful habits and to cultivate attitudes that will lead to higher executive planes. Check lists, rating scales and aptitude tests for executives are all very useful to him, since they enable him to chart both his present position and the direction he must take in the future.

Certain qualities and abilities are bound to stand out among all the others, as he takes stock of what he must do to perfect himself. At the same time, they are the qualities which the understanding employer hopes to see him cultivate. Let us see what some of these supremely desirable traits and abilities are.

7. *Ability to learn*. First, we want to stress the importance of adaptability in the make-up of a junior executive. He is not an independent man working alone. He is part of an organization, taking instructions, giving instructions, working with others; he must adapt himself to his position so there shall be the least possible friction.

The junior executive cannot be a dull man, slow of comprehension. It must not be necessary to explain things to him twice. He must understand his chief's mental habits and modes of expression, and listen attentively to instructions so that no words need be wasted. These requirements mean that he must put himself into the proper adjustment in his relations with his superior. He should be equally adaptable, flexible and tactful in his relations with his equals and with the men whom he commands.

Adjustment to environment has been an important condition of survival in the animal world. The same principle applies equally in business. A man lacking in adaptability or power of adjustment should cultivate if he is connected with a business organization.

The real business man is eager to learn, and willing to use his ears as well as well as his eyes for this purpose. He wants to know the best way of doing things, and he will listen to a visitor, or a speaker at a meeting, or his neighbor at a business dinner, or a fellow-member of a professional or technical society or a club. In fact, he seeks out such contacts-he does not wait for the world to deliver knowledge to his door. No man knows the limits of his intellectual powers, but he may be sure that systematic mental exercise will yield results quite as remarkable or startling as any produced by systematic physical exercise.

Let the junior executive, therefore, cultivate a taste for knowledge. The more he talks with other men about matters of business, and the more he reads and thinks, the better will be his understanding of all that he hears and sees in business, the more constructive will be his service to his company and the more remunerative his progress to himself.

In addition, no matter what his previous education and training, the junior executive should continue to read and study. The world moves on but he will stand still unless he keeps himself up to date on the methods of modern business.

There was a time when "cut and dried" methods prevailed, the ropes could be learned gradually, changes were few and slow, there was plenty of time to correct any mistakes. "Going up the line" was a gradual process, and the ambitious man could soon pass his fellow-workers who were content to plod leisurely along in much the same old rut.

Today, with word flashed to all corners of the globe as soon as an important event happens, with high-speed transportation, and with the multitude of new facilities available to carry on the affairs of manufacturing, trade and finance, business transactions take place between widely distant points and are completed sometimes in moments instead of weeks. There is no time to put a proposition aside until the way to handle it can be learned gradually. Knowledge must be immediately in hand so that action may be taken.

The questions, "What shall I do?" and "How shall I do it?" cannot wait on the tedious processes of learning only by experience. They must be answered by the knowledge of business principles and their applications, and acquaintanceship with successful methods and procedures. Experience need not precede-it must often parallel-knowledge. But the necessity for having the information will not hold off until the years of experience have been obtained.

"Burning the midnight oil" is an old-fashioned term which has become ultramodern in practice. Night classes and home study are profitably utilized by millions of progressive, ambitious men and women today. The largest percentage of successful persons will come from those who have the will power to make good use of their spare time.

8. *Ability to contribute new ideas*. Although the junior executive is not in charge of the major responsibilities of the business, he should not be a business automaton incapable of originality or initiative. It must not be forgotten that he is subexecutive, that in his department he represents those of a higher authority, and that he should be doing there all that his chief himself would do if he were there. If the costs in his department seem out of proportion to results, he must plan for their reduction just as the chief himself would plan. If one of his problems is so baffling that the chief, if it were his problem, would take it home and think of it at night and over the week-end, then the junior executive himself must take it home with him. He must be constantly planning to make his department more efficient-that is, to make results bigger and costs smaller.

Many of the big ideas of business have come from the brains of minor executives or employees. A clerk in a cigar store conceived the idea of the great chain of stores known as the United Cigar Stores. The Woolworth Building in New York City is a monument to the genius and initiative of a young man who was a clerk in a county store when he discovered the commercial importance of the nickel and dime. The history of American business furnishes thousands of similar illustrations of originality and initiative on the part of men who were in subordinate positions when they seized upon a big idea.

The junior executive owes his position to his display of intellectual quality as a worker in some lower job. He knows the steps up which he has climbed. He should know better than anybody else where the effort is wasted, where time is lost, where there is unnecessary friction. His chief, therefore, has a right to expect from him ideas and suggestions that will enlarge the business and enhance the profits.

9. *Teamwork*. A dogmatic, opinionated, obstinate man does not make a good junior executive. He may have a good mind and a

good education, and may know a great deal about business, but he does not pull together with the others. He makes smooth teamwork impossible.

Every business organization is a unit. The various departments should be conducted in harmony with a single plan, as if one mind were in absolute control. If a junior executive thinks that a certain policy is bad and that a change ought to be made, he has the right to argue for his opinion, but if he cannot convince his chief or a majority of the other executives, he must drop the matter and turn his energies toward making the favored policy succeed.

This step some men seem unable to take. A man of that sort clings tenaciously to his opinions and cannot conceal his dissatisfaction when his co-workers do not agree with him and decide to follow a course contrary to his opinion. Such a man is unconsciously capable of serious negligence in a crisis. He never has the entire confidence of his fellows and should not hold a position of great responsibility requiring cooperation with others.

In an ideal business organization, the junior executive pull together so smoothly and evenly that the directing will and purpose of the chief executive are realized in every department, a single mind controlling all. Under such conditions the entire unit moves like a perfectly timed football team.

10. *Loyalty*. A junior executive, possessing the confidence of his immediate superior and entrusted with important responsibilities, must be genuinely loyal. He is the personal representative of his chief and must not be disloyal in word, deed, or thought. He must believe in the business, in the organization, in the chief. His own job must be so inspiring to him that he will understand well what Petrarch meant when he wrote, "I get tired whilst I am resting, and rest while I work. When I take up my work, I fear nothing so much as having to tear myself away from it."

A military leader wants no officers under him who are not patriots, who do not believe in the cause for which they are fighting. A man never fights well unless he is dead earnest. A subexecutive in business, if he is to do his best, must believe in the importance and value of the work he is doing. If he is connected with a business he does not like, or is under a man whom he does not respect, he should look for another connection.

He should take this step both for his own sake and that of his company.

A junior executive lacking in loyalty may make trouble in many different ways. He may talk indiscreetly about the conditions or prospects of the business and give encouragement to competitors. He may even reveal valuable secrets of the business-an act of despicable treachery. His careless words of criticism may arouse discontent among the employees, and chill the enthusiasm of his brother junior executives. A man who is by nature discontented, ultra-critical and self-centered, has not in him the stuff out of which good junior executives are made. It is impossible for such men to be loyal to anybody, or to win loyalty of subalterns to them.

11. *Ability to follow instructions*. Just as the junior executive expects obedience from the men under him so he must follow the instructions of his superiors. The man who cannot control himself and render prompt and willing service to others makes a poor captain and will have weak control of his men. The chief of a business division knows what he wants done and how it ought to be done; he gives the necessary instructions to his subordinates and then turns to other matters, expecting that his orders will be followed to the letter, down the line.

If the subordinate, giving mere lip obedience, pursues a policy contrary to that directed by the chief, thinking that he understands the matter better than his superior because he alone is familiar with all the details, or because the chief was "too busy to get a real grasp of the situation." Sooner or later something decidedly unpleasant will happen. The subordinate will either get a severe reprimand from the chief, or be summoned for dismissal.

No man responsible for the conduct of a business will long tolerate under him men who willfully disobey his orders. Obedience is a primal virtue in business as well as in war. Without it, no business can secure unity of action.

12. *The junior executive's future*. Let us assume that we are considering the career of a typical junior executive. He entered business with some educational background, high school at least, and perhaps college. Whatever the extent of his background, he found that he had much to learn, was in fact a novice. Happily, he was assigned to work under the direction of an understanding man who carefully instructed him in his duties.

He obtained year by year a broader view of the business as a whole and the relationships between departments.

Our novice made good, received promotions and higher pay. To gain a better all-around view of the business, he was transferred to different departments, qualified as a supervisor, and now has been promoted to a junior executive position. He has arrived at the point where he should take stock in himself. Where does he stand?

13. *What has he given the company*? The first question is, "What has he given the company?" This question is settled satisfactorily only if the answer shows more than the minimum requirements. At the minimum level he has given his time, his energy, his exclusive services, and the normal record of punctual arrival and regular attendance. As a maximum, he should be able to register highly in all of the qualities discussed or implied in this chapter. Then he will have earned for the company considerably more than the salary investment in him normally would be expected to return. A worthy management will not forget this agreeable discovery and will reward him properly as opportunity offers.

There are, however, certain other things that the company may now expect of him, if he is to continue on his way upward in the organization.

(1) Has he arrived at his present position only on the momentum of his educational preparation and first start in the company, or is he still "going places" because of alertness and initiative? Is he, figuratively, like a glider floating merely by skillful use of favorable winds and air currents, or is he like a power-driven plane, able to navigate under adverse conditions or to soar to great heights?

(2) Has he kept his "fuel tank" replenished by reading and studying to improve his knowledge of business, to broaden out and to become better informed on his commercial, financial, or technical specialty?

(3) Can he contribute new ideas and suggestions because he continues to think?

(4) Is he a good mixer and does he hold office in business associations, trade or professional organizations, technical or management societies, so that he is in touch with the latest developments and can make use of them on his company?

(5) Does he take part in the affairs of public, beneficial, religious, or social organizations and have standing in his own community?

(6) Is he constructively aiding in the general upbuilding of the company besides running his own department well?

(7) What do his associates think of him?

(8) Is he a leader? Do others rally to him, or do they oppose or "fight shy" of him?

14. *What has the junior executive received from the company*? In return for what he has contributed to the company the junior executive may well ask, "What have I received from the company?" He has received, of course, steady employment, increase in salary, advancement in position, and certain training in the techniques of one or more of the specialized branches of the business.

But there are many more advantages which he should have received and it is will to take stock of them in planning his future course:

(1) Has he been given fundamental training, both in broader business principles and in the line of his field of work, so that he is better qualified by wider knowledge as well as experience to handle larger responsibilities?

(2) Has he been given increasing authority along with his responsibilities, or is management one which begins to withhold authority and a voice in decisions as a man goes up the line, in order not to let him encroach too closely on official prerogatives?

(3) Do officers and higher executives delegate to younger men the jobs demanding for performance the greater vigor and activity of youth, as they should, and retain for themselves only those for which years of seasoned judgement and the prestige of business or professional standing are necessary?

(4) Is the company hidebound by tradition, or progressive, up to date, and ready when opportunity knocks, to change methods, add equipment, and develop new products and markets to arrive at wider distribution, higher prestige, and larger profits?

(5) What are the long-term prospects of the particular business or industry as to markets, profits, salary earnings, and continuance of company existence?

15. *Prospects in the business.* Often a junior executive who has proved his worth in an organization receives an offer of a higher salary from another concern. Shall he accept and leave organization with whose affairs he is so familiar? In no case can we answer the question wisely unless we know and consider all the circumstances.

It may safely be said, however, that no junior executive should resign his position merely because of a tempting increase in salary. There are many things he does not know: Will he fit in with the new organization? Will he be as efficient there as here? Will his ways of doing things satisfy the new chief? Will his prospect of future advancement be as good as now? Is the other business likely to grow or to stand still? Is it controlled by men comparatively young and full of ambition, or by older men already satisfied with the business? Questions of this sort the junior executive must consider before he is in a position to decide upon making a change.

In general, if he is connected with a prosperous, growing business, it is well for him to bear in mind that the world looks with some suspicion upon a man who is moving from pillar to post. When he resigns a good position and goes to another, most people will know merely that he has made a change, and many will suspect that his former employers made it easy for him to leave.

If, however, a junior executive is connected with a business controlled by men who are unprogressive, or incompetent, or lack ambition and initiative, or devote all their time to sports, amusements and travel, and he is convinced in consequence that the business will suffer from their neglect, he is wise if he looks for new connections. It is unfortunate, of course, that he has to make a change, but he has the very best of reasons for doing so. A live man should not be tied to a business that is dying from dry rot.

Advisory 5

Personal Efficiency

1. *Many-sided demands upon the executive*. If the preceding chapters accomplished their purpose, they made clear to the reader the wide variety of tasks assumed by a business executive, either actually in his present position or, potentially, in the positions to which a successful business career is likely to lead him. The many-sided activities of management make heavy demands upon the executives' body and mind, often requiring a degree of physical stamina and intellectual alertness considerably above the average.

To meet these demands, the business man must learn how to keep fit, physically and mentally-even emotionally. His body and mind must be dependable instrument for carrying out his own and his company's objectives. The sum total of his physical, mental and cultural traits should be fused into strong, agreeable personality, enabling him to take the place of leadership that rightfully belongs to the executive.

To some readers, this may appear a large order, and in truth it is. Nevertheless, it is what every man must accomplish if he would be outstandingly successful. He may have initial advantages such as a good heredity, a happy childhood, and a superior education. These advantages may enable him to develop a strong business personality more rapidly than is usual and reduce the pains of growth and development to a minimum. We are reminded, also, that some men, regardless of heredity or education, achieve limited success in business by a process of drifting or "muddling through." They are the opportunists who are shrewd enough to recognize opportunities and take advantage of them.

In general, however, drifting and opportunism are poor methods on which to place one's reliance. They leave to much to chance. They put a premium upon the development of laziness, and encourage attitudes of daydreaming or of defeatism. The drifter either is led to invent face-saving excuses for his lack of success, or he gets in his own way through developing inefficient habits at work.

The right course is resolutely to face the task of developing a maximum personal efficiency. There may be much to do, but the task can be broken down into parts, and one part attacked at a time. "Divide and conquer" was Caesar's prescription for the conquest of Gaul, and it is still a good strategy today. In a large sense, the remainder of this book with be devoted to indicating the objectives and strategy involved in the acquisition of a greater measure of personal efficiency. Thus, separate chapters will discuss the strategy of keeping physically fit, of making the most of one's mind, of developing a strong personality, and so on.

2. *Knowledge and experience are not enough.* First among the demands made upon the business executive are those calling for knowledge and experience. The business man must know, or come to know, the particular field of operations in which he is working. His knowledge of this field must be exact and detailed. In addition, he must have a reliable familiarity with those related departments of the business which affect the success or failure of his own department or division.

Ignorance or inexact knowledge may endanger what the executive is trying to build up, or, at the very least, add an appreciable sum to the unit costs of his departmental operations. Unnecessary costs, of course, whittle down profits.

Moreover, they do not escape the eyes of other executives, including those in the company officers or the board of directors, who quite naturally will seek an explanation. In the long run, there is no substitute for knowledge, and the executive who does not have it, or show himself able to get it, is soon marked for replacement.

Even with knowledge, however, an executive may fail to realize his opportunities through an inability to make the right use of what he knows. This inability usually stems from some defect of temperament or character, from some lack of vision, courage, initiative or perseverance. These larger traits of mind and personality limit the application of the business man's knowledge, setting a stage, so to speak, that may be too large or too small for the operation of his skills and technical information. In particular, the personality traits of the executive determine whether he will be a leader or a follower among other executives, and whether he has the power to lead his company to higher and higher levels of achievement.

Obviously, then, the business man's traits of mind and personality are as much a part of his equipment for handling executive tasks as are his skills and knowledge. They may serve to reinforce experience and knowledge, or, if wrongly developed, may detract from these other assets. It is clear, therefore, that personality traits should not be allowed to develop by chance, but should be inquired into. If inquiry shows the need, they should be corrected or improved.

The encouraging aspect of this matter is that character and personality traits are subject to study and training (or re-training) in exactly the same way that other habits and habitual attitudes are studied and improved. No man should imagine that a job cannot be done, or that he cannot "be born anew." He can, as we shall have occasion to see.

3. *The support of physical vigor.* In some of the charmingly quaint chronicles of medieval saints, the men of God refer to their obstinate, temptation-afflicted bodies by the whimsical name of "Brother Ass." Their idea was that the soul is like a rider, the body a bulky mule refusing to obey his rider's commands. Many a business man has had occasion to sympathize with these medieval complaints against the treachery of the body, which has a way of balking when its help is most needed.

It is true, of course, that Brother Ass could draw an impressive bill of complaints against his rider, starting with overwork, curtailed sleep, irregular meals, too much nicotine or alcohol, and so on. What is needed, obviously, is a more substantial amount of cooperation between rider and body.

There can be no question of the importance of a fair treatment of one's body for the building and maintenance of physical vigor, without which much is lost or never accomplished in business as elsewhere. The salesman, for example, will tell you that his sales have a way of slumping when his health and vigor are below par. "No pep" is his diagnosis, meaning that he is unable to summon his normal driving power and perseverance. At the same time, doubtless, his personality lacks some of its customary sparkle or persuasiveness, for poor health is reflected in a man's eyes, complexion poise and muscular tone.

Business is not transacted in the quiet of a library or with the leisureliness befitting an artist or a philosopher. The artist may paint away at pictures which few understand or appreciate now, and the philosopher may set down his penetrating analysis of the nature of things, both content to let time disclose their meanings to wider and wider audiences. The business man, in contrast, must get results here and now, or slide down the path that leads to bankruptcy. The theater of his activities is more like an arena, where competitors as robust and determined as he dispute his bid for sales.

Winning out against competition, or against the difficulties created by material shortages, labor troubles, inadequate finances and all other obstacles that beset the business man, requires a better-than-average fund of physical energy. If the business man is blessed with a strong constitution from birth, the battle is easier, but even so has his limits.

In a way, the man whose physical heritage has always been only mediocre has an advantage, for he is aware of the need of conserving his strength and replenishing it by sound habits of living, whereas the man born with vigorous health may ignore or neglect these safeguards of energy. In a later chapter, we shall discuss the more important safeguards in detail.

4. *Conservation of energy.* There are all too many ways of dissipating the business man's fund of physical energy, and not all of these sources of waste are physical. Mental efficiency

is involved, and even emotional efficiency. Faulty habits of concentration, of planning, of thinking, or of memorizing can all waste substantial amounts of time and energy. Faulty control of emotions or indulgence in prejudices may waste even larger amounts. And on a physical level, time and energy may be squandered not only on unwise diets and irregular sleep, but also by a poor organization of working tools and routines. A badly organized desk will by itself cut down the executive's efficiency. Illogical office routines will duplicate motions and waste time for an entire staff of executives.

Efficiency may be defined as a form of economy or conservation, since its essence is the economy of energy, time and space. The word comes from the Latin *efficio*, which means, "I do thoroughly, completely, triumphantly." If we think of a man as a bundle of energy, physical and mental, which must expend itself subject to the laws of space and time, the highest degree of efficiency is attained when a given amount of energy is so wisely directed that a task is completed in the least possible space and after the lapse of the least possible time.

A humble but instructive example of efficiency was the housewife of the last century, when women's work was much heavier than now. The word "efficiency" was unknown, but the housewife who took useless steps, or let any time pass without getting something done, sure acquired a reputation for being lazy or "shiftless." She kept the churn and cheese-press near the pantry where the milk was stored, thus saving steps; when she went down into the cellar to get butter or apples, she took with her something that had to be returned to the cellar, again saving steps; and when her morning's work was done and she could rest, she sat down and braided straw hats or knitted stockings, thus saving time.

Efficiency today is a favorite topic of the engineer. He thinks of it as a maximum of result produced by a minimum energy. An engine that utilizes only twenty per cent of the energy in the fuel consumed is said to be twenty per cent efficient, eighty per cent of the energy having been wasted. A machine one hundred per cent efficient has never been invented, and probably never will be, but the engineer nevertheless keeps working on the problem of reducing the waste of energy in every type of machine. A man is infinitely more than a machine, yet it will profit him occasionally to consider his energies and their dispersal as he would appraise the efficiency of any mechanical unit.

5. *The economy of self-organization*. Organization is a vital concern of any business, whether for the company as a whole or for each individual department. Good organization assigns activities and duties so that every department and every individual knows what responsibilities belong to him or his department, how his department is related to other departments, and how the lines of authority run in the business.

But organization and operative efficiency, like charity, should begin at home. The earnest executive will investigate his self-organization. Is he planning and disposing of his own work with 100 per cent efficiency? If self-examination tells him that his efficiency is below the standard he would set for himself, he should check up and start reorganizing.

Poor planning and organization create certain forms of wasted energy and time that are easily recognizable. One waste, for example, is a needless shifting from activity during the business day, so that the executive is in the position of constantly stopping and starting. The human machine, like any other machine, loses momentum when it stops, takes time to regain momentum when it starts up after an interruption. Proper planning will group the major activities of the day or the week so that there will be a minimum of shifting from one line of action or study to another. Planning can reduce much unnecessary back-tracking.

One common fault in executive's self-organization is a habit of doing all the less important things first-a warming-up process intended to carry the executive along until he can really start pitching What actually happens, as a consequence of this poor sequence of operations, is that the executive's most important tasks are postponed and bunched into the busiest hours of the day, when it is hardest to give adequate consideration to them and when their disposal becomes burdensome and fatiguing in the extreme. It is the little jobs that should take second place.

Another error is that of packing the day's schedule so full that there is no free time for emergency problems. The emergencies have to be taken care of, nevertheless, and tomorrow's schedule gets today's unfinished business. Every executive knows that there is a big difference between tackling unfinished business and the business that belongs on today's schedule. The difference is often only psychological, for the "unfinished business" should have been schedules for today anyway, but there is a feeling of hurry that detracts from serene analysis of the problems involved.

Free periods should definitely have a place on the executive's schedule, not only for emergencies but also for minor matters not put on the regular schedule.

6. *How to make a workable schedule.* The business man who wants to make a dependable working schedule should take a leaf from the practice of the personnel manager. A bit of homemade job analysis will solve his problem for him. Let him keep a record over a week-or, better, over several weeks-of everything that he does during the working day. He should include, also, what he would like to do but usually does not find time to accomplish.

A study of the record will show certain activities that repeat themselves regularly and can be grouped together. How much regularity appears in the record may depend somewhat on the nature of the executive's position. Some men have so much regularity that their duties naturally fall into routines. For other men, it may appear at first that only the regular feature if their work is its irregularity.

However, a little study will show that the executive's daily and weekly activities can be classified from one viewpoint to another. Even the junior executive who is subject to calls from his seniors at any hour of the day can make use of the schedule principle. There is such a thing as planning how to meet different kinds of calls-what data to have ready, what materials to take to the superior's office, what method of presentation will save time on a call. The important thing to remember is that calls to a conference are not interruptions of a schedule, but an integral part of it.

If the regular duties of the executive, junior or senior, take him outside his office, either for inspection or consultation, the factor of saving steps and time will enter into the making of his working schedule. If outside trips are numerous, geography may be the dominating factor in schedule-making.

For most executives, however, other factors will be more important. Grouping activities according to the availability of people who must be consulted during the day may be important. Some executives will want to take care of their most exacting duties during the hours of the day when their energy seems to be the most abundant; for other executives, blessed with sturdier constitutions, one hour is as good as another.

Assuming that none of the factors we have just named is dominant, the ideal approach to schedule-making is to group activities according to the nature of the work involved. For example, those involving study, analysis, and decision-making may be grouped together, perhaps in connection with going over the morning mail, or perhaps reserved for the final hour of the day, when the nest day's work should be surveyed at least briefly.

Activities involving the inspection of subordinates' work form a second natural group. They may include the approval of routine reports, telephone calls around the plant to get data on progress, inspections on the job and plant tours, the examining of equipment and giving counsel. A progress chart in the executive's office will show where help is needed.

Consultations may be numerous and frequent enough to form a third group of activities on the working schedule. Such consultations may include reporting to superiors, or general discussion of points of policy, as in a sales meeting or staff conference. Occasionally, some new policy may require explaining to subordinates called together as a group, or departmental meetings presided over by the executive whose schedule we are considering may be thought valuable enough to be put on a regular basis.

When the executive has studied the recorded activities that comprise his working week, and has made some sort of classification or grouping of these activities should be given a regular place in the schedule and which put down for disposal during a "free" period. Each task should be assigned the time it is worth, no more but no less. A good sense of proportion will be developed by experience with working by the schedule.

If trifles have been eating up the executive's time, his study of activities should show it, and undoubtedly will. Concentrating upon the really important tasks can be made a habit, and is habitable with business leaders. One such leader begins his business day by consulting a list, always on his desk in the morning, of "The Ten Most Important Things To Do Today." This approach to schedule-making is feasible even for the man whose main task is "trouble-shooting" and whose time is almost impossible to budget.

7. *Keeping to a schedule.* Theodore Roosevelt was famous in his day as the apostle of the strenuous life. Few people realized, however, that his energetic handling of presidential duties was not a matter of temperament only, but was based on the most systematic organization of his working day. The following description of his daily routine was written by an observer who had access to the White House office:

> Every morning Secretary Loeb places a type-written list of his engagements for the day on his desk, sometimes reduced to five-minute intervals. And no railroad engineer runs more sharply on his schedule than he. His watch comes out of his pocket, he cuts off the interview, or signs a paper, and turns instantly, according to his time-table, to the next engagement.

> If there is an interval left over, he chinks in the time by reading a paragraph of history from the book that lies always ready at his elbow, or by writing two or three sentences in an article on Irish folklore, or bear-hunting. Thus he never stops running, even while he stokes and fires; the engine is always under full head of steam.

Such careful adherence to schedule as this stands the test of results. The man who neglects to plan, or who cannot carry out a plan, tears his way through heaps of correspondence, sends hurry-up calls, answers the telephone, or rushes away to a conference in whatever sequence these tasks force upon him. He complains, quite truthfully, of being "worked to death"; yet, for all his energy, he gets less done than he would like. Because he has no system, or fails to live up to one, he cannot concentrate properly, nor gain perspective. Results are bound to be haphazard and uneven.

8. *The executive's workshop.* An important aid to the following of a schedule is a well-arranged office or a desk, permitting of the forming and continuance of efficient work habits. Thinking of his office as a workshop and his desk as a

work bench, the executive who wants to conserve time and energy will study the present efficiency of his environment and tools. Do they help or hinder? Make steps or save steps? Save time or waste time? It is important to know.

An efficient office arrangement doesn't just happen. To use space and tolls to the best advantage, careful planning is necessary. This is not always given. Executives often inherit offices from their predecessors, and assume that they have planned about as well as can be. A day's record of his motions in his office or at his desk might convince the executive otherwise. A floor plan of his office, with dotted lines showing trips to files or maps or tables, might indicate waste motion in several conspicuous respects. A similar study of what he of what he has to reach for on or in his desk might likewise be revealing.

Not long ago, an executive was notified that his office would have to be cut down in width by eight feet. Before protesting, he decided to study is existing layout. Along the window side of his office he had, in the corner, a bookcase, and between the two windows his desk and chair, with a chair for visitors. Across the room was a table on which he worked out plans, keeping photographs and plans beneath it. There was also a filing case for correspondence and records, and in the far corner stood a collection of rolled maps.

Keeping a record of his motions while in his office, our executive discovered that during two two-hour periods he turned to his bookcase (which was right behind his chair) zero times. He consulted his filing case five times, in each instance to see cards kept in a small 4x6 tray. He walked to the table and back eighteen times, several of these being for tools wanted at the table but kept on the desk. He made four trips to the maps, plus a few others from file to maps, or from maps to table, or from desk to door.

Behind his chair, where the bookshelf had been, Mr. X placed the work table he used so frequently. A small rack added to the table held all the books he really needed. Merely by turning his chair he could work either at his desk or at the table. The 4x6 tray of market data that he consulted once or twice an hour found a new home in a drawer of his desk, saving more steps. The filing case remained across the room, but it was nearer after the office was narrowed. A new wall cabinet was purchased to hold the maps previously allowed to stand in the far corner. The photographs and plans once piled under the table were mounted on display rack, hinged so to swing out as needed.

Net results of the new layout were to give our executive a much more attractive office and one that actually seemed more spacious than before. In addition, valuable time and energy were saved by the changes of furniture, and Mr. X felt a glow of satisfaction from his enhanced efficiency.

9. *Some hints on desk organization*. For many years, a huge roll-top desk was the business man's emblem of authority. Behind its bulky from he conducted his most important conferences; within its multitudinous pigeonholes he hid the firm's secret papers. As office organizations grew larger, the roll-top desk become lower, so that the executive could see what was going on at the desks of his subordinates. Moreover, as filing equipment was improved and made more convenient, there was less need to use a desk for a storage cabinet. The flat-top desk succeeded to the roll-top.

There is a bit of psychology involved in the design of a flat-top desk, which is really a table supported on two pedestals containing drawers. There is no top to shut down finished work, thereby hiding it from the view of associates or superiors, nor are there any pigeonholes wherein to file troublesome papers-out of sight but also out of mind. The flat-top desk suggests a deck cleared for action; unfinished work is an eyesore that the worker hastens to remove, by work, so that he may leave his desk neat and shipshape when the hour comes to go home.

The first rule of desk efficiency is that work should *go across* a desk, never stay in or on it. To treat one's desk as a storage place for documents and records is to mistake its real purpose. Permanent or semi-permanent papers belong in a filing case; only the immediately usable papers pertaining to the day's work should be temporary storage in the desk-these, and the various tools needed to dispatch that work, such as pens, penholders, pencils, rubber stamps. Paste, etc.

The executive's desk should testify to the fact that he is an executive and not a clerk. Material that belongs in the general files should be kept there, called for as needed, and returned promptly when it has served its purpose. Correspondence should be separated from reports, trade journals, and pamphlets. Papers temporarily withheld from the general files should be kept in a tray or drawer where they can be located in the executive's absence if needed by associates.

10. *Desk accessories.* The accessories that are being built into modern desks make it easier than ever for the executive to keep the top of his desk free of unsightly piles of papers. Removable trays are furnished for separating incoming from outgoing mail, or for holding current reports. Removable trays are furnished for separating incoming from outgoing mail, or for holding current reports. Compartments beneath the sliding trays hold letters awaiting dictation and those that are temporarily held up for further information or analysis. This arrangement is convenient for the executive's secretary or for the office messenger service, and does away with the need of letter baskets on the desk top-no great ornament to a desk.

If desired, a quick-reference card file can be mounted in an upper drawer, either for use as a tickler memorandum or for keeping addresses and telephone numbers, prices and quotations, stock and work reports, or whatever information the executive needs to consult frequently. The lower drawers may be had in double-depth, to accommodate a vertical work-file, with folders for the executive's various interests, reports, abstracts of correspondence, and the like.

Another built-in accessory, the removable waste basket, eliminates an unattractive stumbling-block from the modern office. The drawer containing this accessory is not locked with the rest of the desk, thereby allowing the porter to open a drawer and empty the tray that substitutes for the old-fashioned waste basket. This feature is particularly helpful in improving the appearance of an office containing many desks, with their lines of baskets cluttering up the floor.

Certain accessories are standard items of equipment on, rather than in, the desk, such as a good lamp, a convenient telephone, a desk set, and a calendar. Some executives prefer work organizers and memory ticklers on the desk top, rather than a card or vertical files within the desk drawers. A useful variant on the work organizer is the combined desk pad and systematizer, hinged at the center so that it can be folded and carried to a conference. Whatever the executive's preferences among available accessories, he should bear in mind that simplicity is the fashionable note in desk equipment and that accessories should be as few as possible so as to leave the desk top free for use as a working surface. Photos and bric-a-brac on a desk may add to its picturesqueness or to its value as a museum piece, but they scarcely give that streamlined effect which is the hallmark of modernity.

11. *The dynamics of efficiency.* A well-planned office and a well-organized desk are good in themselves, but neither they nor a carefully arranged working schedule will suffice unless the man for whom all these aids are secured has within him the spirit and purpose which alone can justify them. A man's efficiency depends absolutely upon the strength of his purpose. Systems, time-cards, stop-watches, calculated economy of time and effort are as if they were worthless fiddle-faddle unless a man's spirit is blazing with purpose.

The man who drifts and lets himself slip along with the current because he is thus spared the pain of overcoming obstacles never reaches a harbor. A man without a purpose is useless as a ship without a rudder. He accomplishes little of permanent value; his efficiency approaches zero. He may appear to be very busy and active, and possess all the external attributes of the hustler, but his activity is like that if a romping dog or of a two-year-old child, useless because aimless. Find out what a man's purpose is in life and you have the measure of his soul. You have also an index to his personal efficiency. A man of weak will and feeble desire is doomed to be inefficient. As St. Paul would say, he must be converted before he can be saved and become a real man.

Advisory 6

Enduring Business Stress

1. *Physical demands of business*. Few people, except physicians, realize the physical demands which modern business places upon executives and employees alike. Both work under the double load of pressure from above to secure results and the mental and physical exactions of the tasks which they, respectively, are performing. Today, the nervous strain of high-speed production is intense, and the physical drains upon human energy to turn out large quantities of work per day have been appreciably increased. Physical unfitness, unless guarded against, or cured if it has developed, may lead eventually to a serious and sometimes permanent break-down.

2. *What is a strong body*? To the average man the term "bodily strength" is probably more or less synonymous with "muscular strength," and in a limited sense this view is correct. But the man who fondly and complacently regards the

bulging of flexed biceps and overlooks the sagging bulge of his abdominal muscles is taking an incomplete and even dangerous inventory of his physical assets-and liabilities. Balanced and coordinated development of the entire muscular system is essential to perfect health, while heavy overdevelopment of any part in an otherwise poorly developed individual is likely to be detrimental to health. The activity and efficiency of the vital organs of the body are in large degree dependent upon the activity and efficiency of the supporting muscular system.

The abdominal muscles are perhaps the most important, as well as the most abused and neglected, in the body of the average man. The combination of sedentary occupation punctuated by spasmodic outbursts of exercise and overeating, is one not calculated to secure balanced coordination and strength. Too much food, too infrequent and then too violent exercise, constipation and autointoxication-these are the pitfalls into which, any a strong man stumbles. The key window is an unnecessary and dangerous addition to the business man's architecture.

The muscles of the back, from one end to the other, including the neck, are important to your well being and efficiency. The man with chronically weak back muscles and a poorly trussed spine sits uneasily in his chair. His body sags, his stomach bulges, his neck hurts and his head aches. The strong mind and the weak back may be less undesirable combination than the reverse, but it is scarcely more likely to lead to real business success, and far more likely to lead to ill health and misery. Chronic backache is one of the common complaints of the day, and is ascribed by the victim by the victim to a variety of causes any one of which may be correct, for the moment. Essentially, however, the fault (when not due to injury or congenital defect) is to be found in weak and poorly developed back muscles.

The muscles of the lower leg and foot are too often neglected. The arch of the foot is a flexible bridge supported by elastic muscular trusses which go as high as the knee. Other small muscles in the foot itself form a dynamic network of support and strength. Weakness in these muscles, as in the back, leads to pain, not only in the feet but in the knees, hips, back and even the head, with resulting nervous and physical instability of more or less consequence.

Injuries to bones and joints which impose long periods or rest and immobilization always result in weakened supporting structures, of which the muscles are the more important. Every physician understands that restoration of these muscles is essential in order to remove the distressing symptoms which follow these injuries. The symptoms of "chronic sacro-iliac" may be due in part if not entirely to weakened back muscles, initiated by the original injury and prolonged by undue inactivity and pampering. Many men and women suffer from a weird variety of symptoms which stem from weak muscles. In most cases there has been no originating injury, unless neglect or laziness can be called by that name.

A strong body is one which all the muscles, because in daily use and adequately developed, perform their individual and collective functions properly.

3. *Sound nerves*. There are many organic diseases of the nervous system, and most of them are difficult of treatment. It is not necessary for the layman to know anything about these diseases. All he need know is that a man who keeps his body in good condition will maintain a sufficiently stable nervous system to cope with his environment and his business problems.

In our modern competitive, high-speed life, the business man needs a sound nervous system. If his nerves are in bad condition on account of autointoxication, headaches, backaches or footaches, he will be irritable when he should be pleasant, restless when he should be in repose, unsteady and excitable when he should be calm. Bad nerves have shipwrecked many a business.

The health of the nervous system and the health of the body go hand and hand. Poisoning of the body by food or drugs, coupled with inadequate exercise and defective eliminations, is by far the commonest cause of "jumpy" nerves. The pains and the aches of a poorly muscled body, coupled with daily overeating, overdrinking and oversmoking, are the natural preludes to irritability, bad temper, distrust, jealousy, discourtesy and all the other somber attributes of the neurasthenic. Radical and spasmodic attempts to recover by means of drastic abstinence or violent exercise are sometimes resorted to, usually leaving the victim more warn out and jumpy than ever.

The brain is the most important part of the nervous system, and the mind and will are its most important functions. A

105

business man who thinks he can neglect his physical health and yet be as shrewd, far-seeing and resolute as ever, is the victim of a serious delusion. A perfectly well man easily finds his way out of difficulties that would floor him if he were sick or only half well. The man who is not in good physical condition seldom gives birth to a new business idea in business. Not only does he lack imagination, but he lacks also the grit and resolution necessary to carry a new idea into effect.

It should be obvious from what has been said that sound nerves, like sound muscles, will follow naturally upon any plan of living based upon moderation in habits, persistent and intelligent exercise, adequate rest, relaxation and play.

4. *Exercise*. As man grows older, his needs with respect to physical activity change. The strenuous games of youth become less and less desired and desirable. But the necessity for exercise, geared to the physical capacity, remains.

Exercise which is joined with pleasure and fun is of course best. It provides the necessary toning down or rest for the perhaps overused brain and nervous system. Men past middle age should avoid physical competition and content themselves with quieter but equally enjoyable diversions such as swimming, golf, and fishing. Setting up exercises or moderate gymnasium work is definitely beneficial and many men learn to enjoy it. But always remember that any exercise which results in fatigue is likely to be harmful or even dangerous.

Exercise, to be effective, must be undertaken with persistence and regularity. The daily "setting-up" takes but ten or twenty minutes a day, and in lieu of something better, serves the purpose quite well. Do not attempt to catch up on neglected exercise by spasmodic overdoing. The percentages are all against you.

If you have insomnia, try a bit of exercise as a hypnotic. If you get out of bed in the morning still tired, try a bit of exercise as a tonic. If you are constipated and have headaches- but why go on?

If you really want health, you must work for it.

5. *Food*. There are not many business men in the United States who suffer from undernutrition, or lack of sufficient food. There are many who suffer from over-nutrition-too much food. The tired man who follows the old and rayed dictum to

"eat plenty of good food to keep his strength up" is literally digging himself an early grave. Good food, yes, but plenty? Let him first regard his mid-section, and make an honest inventory of his weight. There are very few exceptions to the rule that too much weight means too much food. And there are not many exceptions to the rule that too much weight means a shorter, but not necessarily a happier, life.

One of our large insurance companies spends considerable advertising money trying to teach the danger of excess weight. The company has sound business reasons for attempting this. If only partially successful, such an educational campaign will increase the company's profits by increasing the average life expectancy of its clients.

Excess weight is the one great shortener of life that you can do something about. No one else can do it for you.

There is such a disease as nervous indigestion, but to assume that such is the case without competent medical is folly. Self-diagnosis and self-medication in the face of persistent digestive disturbances is not good business. Some men are naturally thin and under average weight, but enjoy excellent health. But the man who is unaccountably losing weight, and does not feel well, is in need of more expert attention than he can give himself. If he temporizes with food fads, vitamins, medicines, exercises and what not, he may well be heading for trouble.

An early visit to the doctor is much less expensive than a late one.

6. *Drugs.* Practically all drugs, to be effective, must also be potentially dangerous. Self-medication is, therefore, a dangerous practice on two counts. First, the drug itself. Second, a false sense of security. An aspirin for the *occasional* ache or pain, or a mild laxative for the *occasional* overindulgence, may be forgiven. But the habitual use of any drug without medical advice is either silly or dangerous or both.

Vitamins, of which we hear so much lately, are classed as food supplements rather than drugs, but the habitual and medically unadvised use of vitamins can be just as unwise as the indiscriminate use of drugs, if only by providing a false sense of security. Some people are naturally introspective and given to worry about their health. Their anxiety may or may not be justified, but self-medication and delay in seeing a competent physician is a fairly sure method of turning worry into dismal fact.

7. *Cooperating with the doctor.* Many people when consulting a physician, particularly a new physician, seem reluctant or unable to tell the doctor the things he must know before he can make his diagnosis. Some exaggerate the trivial, others minimize the essential, and there are always the few who simply refuse to divulge and useful information whatsoever.

Needless to say, the latter group will get scant attention from any doctor who has work to do. Much valuable time is thus wasted by patients who are unable or unwilling to give simple and direct answers to simple and direct questions. Several visits may be necessary before all the facts come out, to the patient's cost.

Occasionally the doctor, in his hurry and fatigue, forgets to ask the one important question. Some years ago, a man having vague digestive symptoms presented himself to a new physician who had modest pride in his ability in the field of digestive diseases. After several weeks of fruitless questionings and expensive examinations, the exasperated doctor (looking at a vitamin advertisement) asked, "Do you take vitamins?" "Oh yes," said the patient. "I take plenty of them." This story has a happy ending, for the patient got well when he quit self-treatment. The doctor still laughs, but rather glumly, at the joke on himself.

Worry is bad medicine. If you feel sick, let your doctor share the burden. Tell him everything. He can worry for you scientifically and to much better purpose. And even though you are now feeling perfectly well let him look you over now and then. It will give him pleasure to examine and advise a healthy person, and it will give you renewed confidence to be assured that you are fit. It simply is not smart to worry about health and to fear a visit to the doctor. The truth, good or bad, will not be nearly as tough as the worry. Consider the words of the prophet who mourned, "That which feared hath come upon me."

8. *Alcohol and other habit-forming drugs.* The wise physician does not attempt to prohibit, but to restrain; not to coerce by threat or dire prediction, but to guide by reason and example. Much has been said and written, pro and con, about alcohol. After trying prohibition for thirteen years, the

American people concluded that mass production and consumption of alcohol could not fully be prohibited.

Alcohol is a normal product of nature. Its use and abuse have gone hand in hand with the use and abuse of food since the beginning of history. It is regarded by physiologists as similar to food on the ground that it is able to replace food by furnishing heat and energy for limited periods of time. Many hysicians use it in the treatment of illness.

Excessive drinking, on the other hand, whether daily or occasional, is not to be classed with excessive eating, for aside from the immediately poisonous effect of massive quantities of alcohol, there is the danger of becoming habituated to a drug which steadily undermines the will to resist, ending finally in the tyranny of an appetite which too often brings mental incompetence and degradation in its train. Compared with this, the purely physical effects of excessive alcohol are of minor importance.

The same general observations are true of the other habit-forming drugs of a dangerous type, such as morphine. As tobacco, tea and coffee, every man must be his own judge, for with respect to these drugs the doctors disagree. If a man does not use them, the presumption is certainly in his favor.

9. *Right mental attitudes*. Much has been written in recent years about the influence of the mind upon the body, and some extremists go so far as to hold that all disease has its origin in the mind and can be healed by some process of right thinking. We need not here discuss the merits or demerits of any of the modern cults based upon the power of the mind over the body. It is enough for us to know that the mind and body are intimately connected and that each in a mysterious way is dependent upon the other.

A physician tells of an interesting experiment made upon a cat. Fifteen minutes after the cat had eaten generously of raw beef, it was placed under the fluoroscope and its stomach was seen working vigorously and rhythmically while Tabby purred contentedly. Then a door was opened and a dog admitted into the room. Instantly the cat's stomach became rigid, and it did not resume its activities until ten minutes after the dog had been ejected. Here is an illustration of the effect of fear upon the unconscious and automatic activity of a most important organ.

It is certainly important for a man to get right mental attitudes not only towards his own work but toward the world in general. It is important for him to know and be master of himself, and it is also important for him to know and be master of his work or business.

Work that is approached with some vision of its value and meaning will become a pleasure and a privilege, instead of drudgery. The man who comes to his job feeling apprehensive and half-sick is not going to enjoy it or be particularly successful at it. If he has not mastered the fundamentals of his work and fears the daily task that face him, he will develop a mental attitude that sooner or later will affect him physically. He will have "nerves," sleep poorly, eat erratically, and smoke or drink unwisely. The result will be a continuing and increasing feeling of physical and mental inadequacy. The solution to such a state of affairs is first, to get into shape physically, and second, to get busy and study the job.

10. *Relaxation*. Earlier in this chapter we discussed the role of exercise in fostering physical and mental efficiency. But the only kind of exercise that is suitable or safe for the business man or office worker is that which results in relaxation of body and mind and turns worry and fatigue into poise and restfulness. Athletic competition and business efficiency are incompatibles. Games and hobbies, whether requiring mush or little physical activity, that produce pleasure and forgetfulness of the day's worries are not only compatible with efficiency but are, indeed, necessary to it.

The right organization of one's work and working environment, as we have seen in previous chapter, is in itself and easing of tension. Such organization may be acquired by anyone who is sufficiently interested in his work and in his future.

First, organize the day's work so that routine matters are disposed of as they may come up, quietly and without pointless fussing or anger. Second, avoid the appearance of haste or excessive activity; learn to get at the problems at hand promptly, calmly and deliberately. Third, if you find yourself breaking either of the above rules, knock off and sit still for a few minutes, or take a short walk, or talk to an associate about anything but business.

Work handled in this way will be easier, and as it becomes easier in will be pleasanter, and any occupation that is pleasant can be relaxing. You can relax while you work.

William James, a philosopher as well as a physician, had this to say on the subject: "I suspect that neither the nature nor the amount of our work is accountable for the frequency and severity of our breakdowns, but that their cause lies rather in those absurd feelings of hurry and having no time, in that breathlessness and tension… by which with us the work is apt to be accompanied."

11. *Moderation*. This word is nearly synonymous with relaxation in that the latter implies moderation in the expenditure of our physical and intellectual assets. But is it is quite possible to relax immoderately and become lazy and shiftless. Some people do just that, because they "feel tired and need rest." It is quite likely that here is nothing about their fatigue that a little hard work could not cure.

But we are concerned here with moderation as it applies to busy men who have work to do. They seldom complain of fatigue, and when they do, it is not work that will cure them. Nor is it exercise, or play, or vitamins or what not. Until they learn to practice moderation in all things, they are quite likely to be as immoderate in their exercising and play as they are in their work.

Earlier in this chapter we have tried to show that moderation and control of the energy that goes into the daily job will result in an improved output and a happier worker. It is just as true that moderation and control of energy in the form of food and drink that a man puts in himself will result in improved efficiency and a happier individual.

The rise in the mortality rates for certain types of heart disease during the past twenty-five years is disconcerting. Many of the victims of this disease are active and successful business and professional men in their late forties and fifties, and most of them in the prime of life and effectiveness at the time of death. These men have been laying the groundwork for their early passing during their active thirties. They have worked intensely, playing hard and even, and eaten carelessly and heavily, and most of them have smoked incessantly. We do not know exactly what reasons moderation might have accomplished in prolonging the useful lives of those who have gone, but the fact that men with such a background do tend to die early and suddenly should not let us forget that there is a word called "moderation."

This chapter, by the way, has not been written for invalids, but for well men who want to keep well.

Advisory 7

Influential Personality

1. *What is personality*? By the personality of a man we mean those qualities which, singly or in combination, distinguish him as an individual and separate him from the crowd. In a way that no science has explained, a man's personality is stamped not merely upon his face, but on his speech, his walk, his manners. Everyone of us carries a personality trade-mark. Mo matter how we try to hide or disguise it, men of experience will always discern it, and what it stands for.

Personality, at bottom, is the man himself, although it has an external as well as an internal aspect. The physical and surface traits of a man are very important in our estimate of his personality, however grounded they may be in something deeper. It is a question, in fact, whether the surface traits do not constitute the overwhelming influence in shaping a man's personality, or shall we say, in shaping the visible pattern thereof? Certainly, the surface traits are the ones that most people see and comment upon.

Curiously enough, the very origin of the word emphasizes the external aspects of personality. The root word is the Latin *persona*, meaning a mask worn by an actor in a drama. The next step was to call the dramatic character a person, a practice which survives in the use of playbills of the Latin title, *Dramatis personae*, indicating a list of the play's characters.

From the stage, the word passed to the courts, and the Roman lawyers used *persona* to mean the character or social position of a man, together with the rights and duties belonging to that character or social position of a man, together with the rights and duties belonging to the character or station. A man might unite several characters or personae in himself, being at the same time a father and a son, a master and a servant. Modern law has continued to use the word, and even to extend it by regarding a corporation as an artificial person.

2. *The social definition of personality.* Modern thoughts about personality emphasizes its social aspects. Instead of thinking of it as a mystery, or as something entirely inherent in the individual, present-day scholars point out that personality does not and cannot develop in a social vacuum. To think of personality merely as the sum total of a person's traits is not enough; personality is more dynamic than that-is, in fact. Concerned with action and behavior. When any person's actions and behavior, including his physical traits, are a kind to interest and serve other people, they begin to take notice. "There's a man who has personality," they say.

The social definition of personality is of a great importance to us, pointing the way to means of improvement and development. Instead of treating personality as a mystical endowment defying analysis, the social definition of personality enables us to view it as a pattern of habits, attitudes and social relations which can be acquired and altered like other habits and attitudes. A man's personality is something that he can improve, if he wants to. And the clues to improvement he gets from noting the reactions of other people to him-what they think about him, what they like or dislike about his appearance, his manners, his hobbies and enthusiasms.

3. *Influence of the social environment.* So important is the social environment in determining personality that it makes a difference where one lives, or when. The same man might develop a somewhat different personality if he were to grow up in one region of the country than another, or if he had been born a century, or two centuries, earlier. Differing occupations also make for variety, since some occupations give

more opportunities for mixing with people than do others, and hence modify personalities more rapidly.

Throughout the ages, it has been noted that the farmer has a different "character" or *persona* than the merchant, the lawyer a set of traits differing from those of a banker, and so on. Today, with more travel and greater ease of communication, these differences are probably much less distinct, yet we all know of cases in which the occupational pattern persists. We are recognizing such persistence when we say of some of acquaintance, "Oh, he's just a typical farmer." Or might be a "typical" salesman or business man.

To dismiss anyone as "typical" is, of course, to imply a criticism. What we are really saying is that the man referred to has not developed and individual personality over and above the personality conferred by his occupation, or a least that it is not readily recognized. If we cared to make a paradox of it, we might complain that our acquaintance has not developed a *personal* personality. In a sense, this might be literally accurate, and certainly it points to the danger in become so wrapped up in the occupation that a man fails to resist its daily pressure upon its habits and attitudes. Letting routine mold one's personality is as dangerous as it is unnecessary.

4. *The influence of age.* Personality changes with age, and not always happily. Here, too, the personality traits of middle and old age have become sufficiently standardized to be easily recognized, and to become the theme of literary writers, as, for example, in Shakespeare's famous "seven ages of man." In part, these changes are the inevitable accompaniment of bodily changes, as a man takes on the typical physical traits of middle and old age. They can be minimized, and everyone knows men and women who have successfully "kept young" despite their advancing years.

One difference between youth and middle age that is not so readily observed is the change that takes place in their respective evaluations of good personality. A young person is inclined to stress the physical traits in personality-stature, complexion, hair, teeth, dimples and smiles, adding the abilities to dance "divinely," to order a good meal, and to use the current slang. It is easy to caricature this evaluation, but it must be remembered that it has its merits.

By contrast, the middle-aged or elderly person is inclined to think of personality in terms of convenient habits and dispositions-to prefer young people who are quiet, deferential, thoughtful, willing to run errands. If the youth is also a good listener, never tiring of the older person's flow of reminiscences and advice, his personality rating hits the top. This picture, too, is a caricature, but the reader will recognize the element of truth it contains. Let him who needs the warning take heed.

5. *Extremes in personality patterns*. With the respect to intensity, personality patterns run the scale from the negative to the violent or the disagreeable. The man who is only a "typical" mechanic or salesman is lost in his occupational pattern. He is akin to the man (often a very young man) whose personality traits are so subdued as to baffle the observer's analysis. He is labelled as a having a negative personality, or as "lacking personality."

In some cases, it may take considerable exploring into the social environment, including the man's home life, before an explanation can be found for the negative personality. In most cases, however, it may be assumed, with reasonable safety, that what is lacking is sufficient participation in recreations and hobbies giving contacts with other people. Personality is not easily developed in solitude. Playing a lone hand leads to introversion, repressions, the growth of anti-social traits. Whenever possible, hobbies and recreational interests should be chosen for their facilitation of social contacts-the more people we meet, the more diverse the personalities we learn how to get along with, the better. That might be called the golden rule in transforming a negative personality into a strong one.

It is to be hoped, of course, that the strong personality will also be an attractive one. This is not always the case, for occasionally we meet a man whom we shall not easily forget, who most certainly has impressed us, but who has aroused only feelings of resentment and dislike. The aggressive, domineering personality, careless of the rights or even susceptibilities of others, is an extreme to be avoided at all costs. His gains from aggressiveness of that type are short-term; his losses, long-term and permanent.

6. *Disagreeable personalities in business*. It is only natural that business men, being so numerous, should include in their company certain types of personalities that are

disagreeable to meet and do business with. The personalities in question are types in that they recur frequently enough to be noted and classified as such. A few examples will suffice.

First, there is the big "I," the pompous man who seeks to impress you with his own importance. Such a person may be suave and dignified, or he may be over gruff and dictatorial. He may make you feel small, or he may just disgust you. At any rate you leave his presence hoping that you will never have to meet him again. In the language of the street, he is the "chesty guy." He is never popular.

Then there is the opposite type, the wheedler, the flatterer, the man who professes to think you are "it" and that he is nothing. He is the counterpart of the "humble" Uriah Heep in Dicken's *David Copperfield*. Self-respecting, sensible people do not like to do business with such men.

Finally, there is the ultra-suspicious man. He is an animated question mark, insisting upon all sorts of information before he will do business. He prides himself upon his intelligence and far-sightedness, and always acts as if afraid that you are trying to deceive him. When a business man lets his fear of trickery completely dominate his character and conduct, and one which is a serious detriment.

7. *Good personality requisite in business*. It would be impossible to describe the many ways in which personality of the right sort is helpful to a man in business. A negative or disagreeable personality is a handicap to the business man in his contacts with the trade, with his associates and employees, and with the community of which he is part. The executive with a fine, strong personality commands respect and good will, accomplishes much for the good of his business and for that of his community. He is welcome everywhere, because he inspires confidence and hope. It may be said of him, as has been said of a modern philosopher, that when he enters a room, it immediately lights. His associates anticipate his opinions with interest and often pleasure.

Business men have themselves stressed the importance of a good personality by their practice in judging applicants for a position. Letters of recommendation count for less with the, than the applicant often imagines. Let ten men answer an advertisement, all but one having excellent references. If the personality of that tenth man is most attractive, the chances are that he will get the job, although always with the condition that, upon investigation, his statements about himself are fully confirmed.

Is this attaching too much importance to personality? Some readers may think so, yet statistical studies support the business man. For example, of 4,000 office and clerical workers discharged by 76 business firms, only 10 per cent were let fo for lack of skill or knowledge. The rest were dismissed for carelessness, laziness, or inability to cooperate-in other words, for remediable faults of personality.

The head of the placement bureau at a midwestern university, speaking from experience, has this to say: "Literally hundreds of graduate students with A and B records, with good training and with the support of many faculty members, still are undesirable in the eyes of the prospective employer, because of incapacity to adjust themselves and because of underdeveloped or peculiar personalities." An official of the American Institute of Banking has stated that "bad manners, bad personality and bad character traits have lost more jobs for beginners in commercial positions than have lack of ability or mechanical skill."

On the positive side, studies of the careers of college graduates show that those who were rated high in personality were the ones to get and hold the better paying, more responsible positions.

8. *"Even your best friend won't tell you."* This slogan, made famous by the advertisements of a mouth-wash manufacturer and referring to unsuspected halitosis, is recalled here to stress a point suggested by the statistics on dismissals quoted above. The point is this: employers rarely give their real reasons when dismissing an employee for faults of personality. If he is told anything, his dismissal is likely to be blamed on "business conditions," "the need for retrenchment," or something equally euphemistic.

If an employer could afford to be absolutely honest about it, he might tell the junior executive about to be discharged something like this: "Smithers, you know a lot about exporting, for a young fellow, and I know it will be hard to replace you, but I just can't stand that asinine simper of yours, nor those long sideburns, nor those foreign phrases you are always throwing at us. Moreover, you waste hours in arguing about the most trivial details, until you have gotten all your associates on edge, and the whole department is irritable and losing its morale. This place just isn't big enough for a guy like you."

The boss can't bring himself to say anything like that; instead, he tells Smithers that export prospects are not so good, the budget must be pared down, and everybody knows how easy it will be for him to make another connection. And so Smithers collects his two week's advance, and goes, a little pale and wondering.

The fact (and it is a fact) that a man may lose his job without learning the real reason, is enough to make almost anyone stop and consider. To make things more difficult, personality faults are not precisely self-evident to the man who has them-at least not all of them for himself.

9. *The discovery of personality traits*. Anyone who is in earnest will find that there are more helps available for the discovery of personality faults then he had supposed, and available without embarrassing either himself or his friends. Personality problems have long been the subject of serious study and investigation by psychologists, psychiatrists, vocational advisors, personnel managers, and other professional men, and there is now considerable literature on the subject.

Any public library can furnish the inquiring executive with an introduction to this literature, either by lending books and magazines or by compiling a bibliography of recent books obtainable through a bookstore or direct from publishers. Some of these may be of a professional or technical nature, written for psychiatrists or personality counselors, and hence not useful to the ordinary inquirer. A few minutes' examination of titles at a good bookstore will suffice to eliminate the technical books, as also those for high school students, leaving the inquirer with a choice of titles suitable for him. He should take only what he likes.

The public library is usually a good place, also, to inquire about educational facilities bearing on personality improvement. Classes in personality development, practical psychology, speech correction, public speaking, posture and poise, and corrective gymnastics are offered by extension departments of local or nearby colleges and universities, b organizations like the Young Men's Christian Association, by professional and business clubs, or even under private, commercial auspices. Checking up on what the local community has to offer may surprise you.

10. *Personality tests*. Some of the books on personality improvement carry suggestions for taking an inventory of personality traits and habits, often in the form of fairly elaborate check list of desirable and undesirable characteristics. These are helpful to the extent that they assist in discovering unsuspecting habits or traits which the man who is earnest would not want to continue with if he could possibly be rid of them. Such lists also build up a detailed picture of what other people regard as a good or a poor personality, and thereby help to point the inquirer's own standards a little higher, or perhaps give him an ideal to aim for.

Rating scales and personality tests more elaborate than check lists, and tested for scoring results on hundreds or thousands of persons, have been devised and published by universities, consulting psychologists, and the Psychological Corporation, New York. Most of these are not for sale to the general public, since they require a psychologist or other properly qualified person to administer them. Such scales and tests as are incorporated in non-technical books on personality improvement are, of course, capable of being self-administered by the intelligent reader. The professional tests can be experienced by seeking admission to a clinic or class in personality improvement.

It is often a surprise to the inquiring business man to discover what a variety of sub-tests is included in a full-fledged personality test. It is really a battery of tests, designed to measure the development of some particular trait or set of skills needed for a good personality. Thus, one rating scale attempts to measure eight characteristics: dependability, cultural refinement, leadership, industriousness, mental alertness, thoroughness, personal grooming and personal appearance. A person's score is the average of the showings made on all eight sub-tests. Other personality tests measure reaction times, participation in community groups and institutions, range of activities and interests, emotional outlets, versatility, reading habits and choices, general knowledge, submissiveness or dominance, introversion or extroversion.

Experience has shown that personality tests, used along with other types, such as aptitude tests, save time and money in business and industry. During a great war, when time and personnel are lacking for interviewing and training the flood of new employees required for producing munitions and military equipment, tests are profitably employed to weed out unsuitable applicants for jobs, and to place those accepted in the positions where they will do their best work. Selective tests, including personality tests, are scarcely less needed in a time of peace.

11. *Improving physical appearance.* Whatever aids may be employed to uncover personality faults, it may be assumed that the faults discovered will include a few that belong in the class of physical deficiencies. Some of these cannot be remedied. No amount of taking thought will change a short man, for example, into a tall one. Nevertheless, a man need not worry about his stature. Mere physical height, or bulk, is not essential to the possession of a strong personality; moral and mental characteristics are much more important. Moreover, other physical traits can be so managed as to offset shortness or baldness or irregular features.

It is true that the tall broad-shouldered, well-muscled man may have a certain initial advantage over a smaller man, but this advantage is short-lived if the personalities of the two men are otherwise balanced equally. It is a matter of record, moreover, that some of history's most influential characters have been men of short stature and even of frail physique. The same is true of facial beauty, which is normally yet not inevitably an asset. A man who is positively homely may nevertheless be more magnetic than a characterless Adonis. Deficiencies in physical endowment can be compensated for by cultivating other attractive traits, such as poise and good posture, courteous and tactful manners, conversational skill, and a general enthusiasm and alertness.

These are worth while in themselves. However, a man need not accept his facial features and general endowment in a fatalistic spirit. Complexions can often be improved through an improved diet, or a regimen of exercise. A change of barber may make a difference-an air of alertness may depend on a new style of haircut. Teeth can be straightened, eyes cured of distressing watering or bloodshot appearance, and so on. A man may be born with unattractive features but he does not have to keep them 100 per cent intact-not all of them at least.

How we dress is a part of the general picture of how we look, and important, as everyone knows, in forming the impression that we make upon other people. Inasmuch as the reader has in all probability long since acquired a sufficient fund of information about the care of clothing and his general grooming, it is necessary to do more than remind him of their contribution to personality.

The way we walk, the way we handle ourselves, and the way we talk are three other important elements in the total impression we make on others. A private session before a full-length mirror will reveal any negative faults of stance and poise. Gestures are a liability to some men because of being awkward, futile, or too frequent; they, too, will bear critical inspection. Uncorrected, they will continue to annoy and drive away associates and customers. A well-pitched voice and good speech habits are an asset to any man. It is astonishing what a little training can do toward developing an attractive voice.

Fundamental to every element of physical appearance is man's state of health. Good health radiates in eyes, in complexion, in voice, and in muscular movements; has something to do, apparel experts say, with the way we wear our cloths. Conversely, a lack of muscular tone and vitality, even though short of ill health, conveys a subtle air of languor or perhaps an ill-concealed irritability to those who are forming their impressions of what we are like. Take care of your health if you want an attractive personality.

12. *Cultural and intellectual factors*. In the sum total of those personal traits which constitute our individuality to others, traits of mind and culture are likely to vie with physical features for attention. In some persons, indeed, the almost dwarf the physical features, completely winning the respect and affection of those who came into their presence. Thus, a man of great intelligence, with an ability to grasp and convey the full breadth of a project or problem, or to indicate original and hopeful solutions, and to do this consistently, is bound to impress others with the quality of his mind. So, too, will the man who has imagination enough to enter sympathetically into another's situation and visualize his needs and problems. Or it may be that a man will impress others by the smooth efficiency with which he plans and carries out his business

tasks, day in and day out. In all these instances, men establish what we may call an intellectual personality. Indeed, we all establish one, regardless of our position in the scale of intelligence or culture.

It is unfortunate, of course, if the cultural traits which we impress upon others as being most typical of us, do not happen to be traits that we can be proud of. Bad speech habits, faulty grammar and a limited or slangy vocabulary are examples of such traits. Grammar is merely a matter of social usage, changing from century to century, and reflecting nothing important as to either character or intelligence, yet nothing is longer remembered by some people than a bad slip in grammar. So, too, for spelling. The person who cannot spell is constantly under-appraised by those who read his messages.

The fact that in business so many people never meet us in person but form their ideas of our personality from our letters, should warn us against carelessness in our use of English and in the analysis of customers' needs and desires. We cannot afford to read the customer's letter so hastily as to miss his point and overlook parts of his message. If we do, our reply will fail to satisfy and will probably even irritate him. "Inefficient" will be his mildest label for our intellectual personality.

Other labels, equally derogatory, will be evoked if what we write is neither clear nor pertinent. Rambling sentences, made more obscure by misplaced modifiers or by pronouns lacking any clear reference, will draw a verdict of mental incoherence. A letter full of short, choppy sentences, with never a subordinating clause, will make the reader wonder whether its author is quite mature. Children treat all their ideas as equally important, but adults are supposed to discriminate.

Again, a letter written in "telegraphese," as if the writer were composing a telegram, omitting subject, pronouns, verbs and anything else that can be left out and still convey a message, will give its reader an unpleasant impression of the author's personality. "Here," the reader will think, "is one o those egotistic, gruff fellows who snap at you. No courtesy is to be expected from this petty tyrant; let's avoid him." The impression may be quite wrong, but the harm is done.

Vocabulary is important. If our ideas are couched only in trite and "rubber-stamp" words and phrases, we either impress the reader as having no personality at all or as being tiresomely conventional. A friendly, persuasive, sales-making personality cannot shine through a mess of quasi-legal jargon and full phrases.

13. *Emotional factors*. Just as buoyant good health infuses a glow into the physical appearance of a man, so certain emotional resources suffuse his intellectual personality. Enthusiasm, sympathy, and optimism ass force and charm to his ideas and projects, and the people who deal with him feel an emotional contagion that is difficult to resist, if, indeed, resistance is needed. Contraiwise, the absence of these positive emotional traits and their supplanting by aloofness, suspicion, or pessimism, will chill and repel.

If the outstanding emotional traits of a man show themselves in fairly consistent patterns, we say that he has a certain kind of temperament, or, more briefly, we pin a label on him. The label may be complimentary, as when we say that Smith is "a good fellow," or it may be an uncomplimentary epithet of a slangy sort, as when we dismiss Smith as "an old grouch."

This recognition of the existence of emotional temperaments should be carried farther. Actually, we are all bundles of emotions and feelings, and what thinking we do is seldom coldly logical. Some men, indeed, may be said to think more with their glands than with their brains, since their opinions and decisions are so often based on feeling or prejudice and are so little the product of any logical process. Nor are such men invariably wrong in their opinions or decisions; they obey deep-seated impulses or "drives" in their nature, subtly-and sometimes correctly-warning them of danger ahead or hinting of a profitable deal in the offing.

Following a "hunch" or obeying intuition may be the only course of action when circumstances are too obscure or confused to be reasoned about, but as a rule intuition is safer a guide for business man than it was for Adolf Hitler, posing as a military strategist. A "hunch" is no substitute for research. And neither, we may add, is a prejudice or what psychiatrist calls a "complex."

14. *Tyranny of the complex*. In the abstract, a complex is a harmless affair, being merely any group of ideas held together by some strong emotional bond. The ideas and memories comprising our experience with life tend to form themselves into

124

groups, bonded by such emotions as family affection, love of the soil, admiration for certain types of men, loyalty to church or nation, etc. In that sense, complexes are the normal result of mental growth and experience; we all have them, and have had them since we were able to react to any experience whatever.

That is not the usual connotation of the word. In practice, the complex has acquired a negative flavor, indicating a trouble spot in the personality. To say, loosely, that a man has a complex about a subject is to warn that he has an exaggerated prejudice or fixed sensitiveness about it. Such a complex cannot be reasoned away, but must be discounted or allowed for in getting the victim's views. If the complex involves an irrational and persistent fear of something, the psychiatrist calls it a *phobia*.

In general, of course, the complexes or prejudices of normal men are neither as persistent as the phobia nor so exaggerated as to be beyond reasoning with, unless the emotion of fear is involved. Still, they do not aid in the business man in his thinking if they really belong in the category of prejudices, and occasionally they may cause him a business loss. If relatively harmless, a man's parade of prejudices may afford amusement, but then he is likely to be depreciated as eccentric or as a sad example of "crabbed old age." The man who deliberately cultivates his prejudices is in reality the victim of a perverted vanity. He craves public attention-at any price.

There is another negative form of complex which is more serious. It is the repressed or unconscious complex-a system of desires and memories which is disguised form come to exert a dominating influence upon the personality. The most common example is the inferiority complex, a much abused term, really referring to an unconscious or disguised motivation of action. Because he secretly doubts his own ability, the victim of this complex either evades as many responsibilities as he can, or bolsters himself by much boasting, or by bullying those under his authority.

Another common complex is the mother complex, by reason f which a son yields and undue obedience to the wishes of a selfish mother, long after the age when he should have learned to make his own decisions and assume a reasonable independence of maternal care. Where the mother is to blame, her fault show itself in an unwillingness to let the boy become a man and begin living his own life. Often, however, it is the boy who has learned to like the prolonged dependence upon "Mom," and to avoid assuming responsibilities that threaten an end to his careless pleasures.

15. *Running away from difficulties*. The more serious forms of complex may not trouble the normal business man nor handicap his personality development, yet none of us is entirely immune from a certain amount of evading or flouting the unpleasant.

For example, if you are thwarted in your desires, do you swear or fume or throw things? Do you ever kick a chair that has gotten in your way? Do you ever imitate the tennis player who hurls his racket to the ground when the game goes against him? If so, you are indulging in what the psychiatrist calls "regressive" behavior, that is, you are reverting to the reactions of a child when confronted by an obstacle. Not very dangerous, but not a great help in winning respect or popularity. To reveal yourself as a child is to invite being treated as a child.

Regressive behavior is more a way of expressing one's dislike of difficulties than of running away from them, but consider the case of the man who is continually "passing the buck," that is, blaming his failures upon some person or thing outside himself. The psychiatrist calls this the "projection" of difficulties. It is a cheap way of purchasing temporary relief from the humiliation that would normally follow the exposure of our own errors. Consistently indulged in, the projection of difficulties gradually widens in its scope until we have made a scapegoats of the majority of our associates and a multitude of individuals outside the company. The government, the business world, perhaps even the economic order, assume the character of conspirators against us. Pessimism and cynicism come to rule our thinking.

Blaming others for our mistakes leads naturally to a closely related method of escaping from difficulties, the method of "rationalizing" them, or inventing convenient reasons to explain our failures. Thus, the man who drops a project because it has turned out to be more burdensome or expensive than he foresaw, instead of admitting the real reason, tells his associates that he never intended to carry it further, or that he only wanted to let them learn by sad experience the project's worthlessness.

A tyrannical office manager enforces severe discipline "for the good of the company," whereas his real reason is that he knows no other way to get along with subordinates, or fears to lose their respect by appearing too human, or, still worse, gets a secret satisfaction from making others miserable. Much more harmless to personality development, of course, but still of no great assistance, is the self-deception of the man who uses and excessive amount of company time in attending luncheon conferences, entertaining out-of-town customers, or "making contacts" on golf courses.

16. *Extrovert versus introvert*. So much has been said or written about this famous distinction as applied to personalities that not much need be added. It is easy to overwork the distinction. Most of us show both extrovert and introvert traits, but it remains true that for many men one or the other kind tends to dominate. The salesmen is still the typical extrovert; the research man, the typical introvert.

Summing up roughly, the introvert is supposed to be "the man of thought"; the extrovert, "the man of action." Introverts like to work alone, shun publicity, make few acquaintances. Extroverts seek companionship and enjoy publicity, get their information from people rather than from books or technical journals, make decisions quickly after a minimum of reflection. Introverts do the inventing, extroverts the promoting.

Both are needed. This needs stressing, since an impression has gotten around that introversion is the next thing to a disease or is at least a symptom of impending mental trouble. The truth is that there is nothing wrong with being either an extrovert or an introvert, unless carried to the extreme. The business world needs both types, the inventor and the promoter.

One caution should be added: either introversion or extroversion may be used to run away from difficulties. Thus, the man with a problem he does not want to face may throw himself into all kinds of business and social activities so that he will have no time left for thinking about his problem. This is what psychiatrists call "the flight into extroversion"-a flight from the unpleasant ordeal of facing or solving a problem. The introvert running away from a problem has another form of escape-he broods or daydreams. He may begin by trying to reason out a solution for his problem, which is wholesome enough, but when he finds it difficult he postpones making a decision, and there real trouble begins. He continues to think beyond the point of fruitful analysis; he goes over the same ground endlessly. Perhaps worse, he imagines a solution that would be possible if the conditions were different; he builds himself a noble castle in Spain. But the real problem remains. All he has done by his brooding or daydreaming is to make it harder to exercise his will and make a decision. Even a bad decision would be better than none.

17. *Be honest and confident*. It was a wised philosopher who gave this rule to his disciples, "Know thyself." However difficult this task may have seemed to the young men around Socrates, it appears many times more formidable today, in the light thrown by modern psychology and psychiatry on the complexity of the human mind. Nevertheless, it is clear that we cannot get far with personality development unless we make a reasonable effort to know ourselves as we really are, with the real motives-good and bad-that underlie the generality of our actions. It is more pleasant to ignore some of these motives and habitual attitudes, but ignorance and self-deception are barriers, rather than aids, to the development of the sort of personality we have set out to win for ourselves. It is more profitable to give up the pleasure of "kidding" ourselves.

This discussion of the emotional factors in personality has not been intended to make any reader beat his breast in humiliation and contrition, nor lead him into investigations having those results. In the competitive world of business, the man who intends to succeed must be unemotional even about the emotions. He may note that he has tended to indulge in regressive behavior, or projection, or rationalization, or excessive extroversion or introversion. Having discovered the tendency, he proceeds to take the appropriate countermeasures, and to go on with his job. He knows that in time, by dint of patience and perseverance, he can substitute more helpful motives and actions for the ones that do not aid in his growth. He loses no time in self-pity or brooding.

The successful business man builds up a trust in his own judgment. If he makes a mistake, he makes it honestly, assumes the consequences, and learns from the experience. He is careful to get all the knowledge he can, to train himself in the best methods available. These are the bases for self-confidence, a confidence which is entirely reasonable and therefore far removed from an odious conceit. And this reasonable confidence

becomes a dominating trait in his personality, and makes him a
leader.

Advisory 8

Teamwork Harmony

1. *The business team.* The concept of the business team is important, and in previous chapters we have laid considerable emphasis upon its necessity. Teamwork and harmonious cooperation are essential to the successful operation of a business. Personalities may sometimes clash, but they cannot be permitted to continue in conflict to the point where cooperation becomes impossible.

Although executives often hold strong opinions as to what the business should do or leave undone, they recognize that all differences are subject to discussion and eventual compromise. The tacit understanding is that decisions must be reached, and once reached, must be loyally adhered to. Differences of opinion must be dropped when the policy has been set. To carry it out, the team must henceforth pull together. If even one member of the team holds back or fails to pull his load, the company's determined purpose may be wrecked.

If teamwork is this important to a going business, it is clear that we should understand thoroughly its nature and development. It is not safe to take teamwork for granted or to assume every executive understands what is involved in the mechanics of giving and securing cooperation. Good intentions and lip service to the ideal of teamwork are not enough; the business executive must know and apply a considerable amount of practical psychology if he is to secure maximum cooperation from associates and subordinates. To rely on good intentions alone is to court shipwreck on unseen reefs of misunderstood human nature. As a matter of fact, a substantial number if failures in management occur from the executive's ignorance of how to work with others and how to get them to work with him.

2. *Three levels on which we work with others*. The simplest analysis of the cooperative situation will disclose three levels of relationship within the business team, as that is usually constituted. The levels are:

(1) Working with superiors.

(2) Working with associates.

(3) Working with subordinates.

The cooperative situation is a little different on each of the three levels, calling for the development of attitudes and methods appropriate to each. Before discussing these special methods, however, we shall consider certain techniques and attitudes that apply to all three levels with roughly the same pertinence.

3. *Cooperation begins at home*. Doing a variation on the ancient adage that "charity begins at home," we may seriously consider whether a program to promote better teamwork should not begin with our own selves. Perhaps the best advice to follow in that connection would be this: "Keep your own personality normal." Avoid extremes; don't overdevelop your personality. The well-balanced man holds his emotions in check, especially when they are of the negative type. He may not be able to help disliking some people, but he cleanses his mind of unfriendly feelings toward them as fast as he can. Acting as if he liked the people who repel him, he often finds that the responses evoked change his own feelings. The unlikable fellow turns out to have a good side to him, unseen at first. Perhaps he, too,

is changing *his* opinion, since the people *we* dislike, will dislike us.

The well-balanced man stands guard over the development of his personality. He does not let his strong points develop to excess, so as to become in any way eccentric or temperamental. He prefers other pleasures to that of playing the prima donna, that is, of letting himself go, regardless of the feelings of others. He does not make bids for sympathy, play "hard to gt," or pretend to be what he is not. He does not need these props to vanity, and recognizes them for what they are-props and masks of the man who is afraid to be himself.

Developing balance in no counsel of perfection, but a practical necessity in business life. It is important, for success, that people should like you; otherwise, you will secure little spontaneous cooperation. A sharp tongue, a callous disregard for the rights and feelings of others, eccentricities conscious or unconscious-all these prevent people from liking a man, or at least make it harder. If enough people dislike a man, his chances for failure increase alarmingly.

4. *Cooperation cannot be commanded*. Cooperation is not something that can be secured by a mimeographed order from the front office. People may go through the motions of cooperating through compulsion, from a motive of fear, but the quality if such cooperation leaves much to be desired. The spirit is out of it, and it is the spirit-the willing attitude-that counts.

Securing cooperation is largely a job for the individual. It is true that morale may be stimulated by mass appeals taking in an entire office, plant or company, as in sales contest or an interplant competition. But these are special efforts, put forth only at intervals, and they leave the individual just where he was, facing the never-ending problem of working with superiors, associates and subordinates.

Getting other people to work with you, rather than against you, is a matter of practical psychology-of arousing their desire to play ball because they see a definite benefit therein, either for themselves or for the company, and hence indirectly for themselves. People are necessarily interested, above all other things, in their own welfare and progress, and their cooperation will be secured in full measure only when they see how a given project will benefit them.

It is easier to convince others that they should give cooperation if they like you. That is because they trust those whom they like and admire, and are not suspicious of their motives. Sometimes, in a pinch, they want to help you just to see you out of a hole. These "personal reasons" for cooperating may not always be entirely logical, but they are nevertheless often the motives that get tangible results. They cannot be commanded, please note, but must be earned.

5. *Build on similarities in others*. The psychological task of gaining cooperation will appear easier if we focus our attention on the similarities in human nature, rather than on the differences. The latter have been overstressed in recent years, owing to the discoveries of the experimental psychologists and the physiatrists, which pointed to the neglect of individual differences in the old-fashioned psychology of earlier centuries.

Important as individual differences are, they are only half the story. The other half is that people share many traits and habitual responses in common, as also the same motivations and desires. They are all interested in what affects their own interests; they want many of the same things from life; they react in much the same way to friendliness, sincerity, and sympathetic understanding. It is because of these positive similarities that you can approach people at random and apply the same procedures with a reasonable assurance of success. The procedures, of course, must be based on tested experience and psychological understanding, whether your own or some one else's.

6. *Procedures that work for everyone*. Examples of well-founded procedures for approaching other people are not difficult to find, and are usually so simple that the only surprise is that they are ever neglected. It is, or should be, axiomatic that anyone approaching another should display friendliness, even when something has gone wrong and regardless of personal feelings. Without being a professional back-slapper or a bone-crushing handshaker, it is possible to give a hearty greeting and show genuine pleasure in seeing the people you meet. The effects are usually twofold; you do yourself good, and you create an atmosphere favorable to cooperation. People respond to friendliness when it is consistent and sustained.

Another simple procedure is to avoid setting the stage for battle. Keep in mind that arguments are rarely held to an intellectual level but quickly involve the irrational emotions. No one likes to lose a contest, and that is what an argument is- a contest. "The desire to be important," says the philosopher, John Dewey, "is the deepest urge in human nature." You may build up your own self-esteem by winning arguments, but if you win at the expense of hurting another's pride, your victory may only be superficial.

Men who are quick at repartee are often prone to exhibit their ability in ways that trample on the pride of their associates. Sometimes the slower thinker comes through with the right solutions, but even if he doesn't, his public discomfiture will rankle and build precisely the wrong atmosphere for cooperation. To force a man to "eat his words," to proclaim publicly that he is wrong, to whittle him down while building yourself up-these are the unforgivable sins against the ideal of a company team. They are all the more reprehensible if committed casually and unnecessarily. They violate the fundamental principle that every man should be shown the respect due him as a person.

7. *The other fellow is egocentric, too.* You are the center of your own mental world, but the other fellow is king over his own realm. He *may* become interested in you, but that interest cannot compare with the concern he feels for his own self-preservation and welfare. To get him to work with you, you must contrive ways of putting him into the center of the picture. He will serve the more if you can build up his self-respect and help him to identify himself importantly with the project in which you are interested.

To do this, it is essential, first of all, to see the other fellow's viewpoint. What interests of his would be served by him cooperating with you? Would any interests be jeopardized, or seem to him to be endangered? Concentrate on ways of meeting the objections he might have. If necessary, modify your project a bit. Prepare to arouse his desire to cooperate; outline a selling plan that will picture clearly what *he* will get from cooperation. Plan your approach so that you will say something the other fellow wants to hear. Step by step, lead him into the center of the picture, where you are. Let him stand beside you.

A good story is told of Samuel Vauclain, who became president of the Baldwin Locomotive works. In his earlier years, he was directed to move tenants from a residential area in Philadelphia that had been bought as the site for new office building. Of the more than 100 tenants, only a handful refused to go. There was no time for court action, and Vauclain decided to see what he could do with the stubborn old Irishwomen who was the group's spokesman. He found her sitting on her doorstep.

"What's ailin' ye?" was her greeting.

"Why shouldn't I be ailing," replied Vauclain, "after all the trouble you have stirred up for me?"

"'Tis your own fault, it is," insisted the Irishwoman.

"Maybe so," said Vauclain then added: "But it's a shame you sit here and do nothing, when you, with your personality, could persuade your neighbors to move to much better houses."

The compliment won the lady over. She became the busiest woman in Philadelphia, bossing her neighbors around until she had moved the whole colony at half the expense Vauchain had expected to incur. He had gotten her to do what he wanted by putting her into his picture in an important way. In a sense, she had become his executive assistant.

8. *Persuasion and discussion are techniques*. Showing another person how he belongs in any given picture may involve the skillful use of persuasion and discussion. Unskillful discussion usually leads to bickering, the poorest atmosphere for winning cooperation. What is needed is the habit of seeking interests and advantages that are common to two persons or two departments, an of stressing what is mutual in the situation. Exploring the possibilities in a friendly way, frankly facing the facts as they are without glossing over the difficulties, but holding fast to the purposes and advantages common to both parties, the skillful negotiator can usually secure a partial agreement sufficient to get action. The rest can be worked out as the project develops.

A little persuasion is often needed after a project has been explored for its mutual benefits. At this point, the art of salesmanship will prove effective. The negotiator must visualize the picture vividly for the other party, show him again what he or his department or the company has to gain by the proposed policy or project, arouse his desire through appeals to such motives as the gaining or loss of prestige and influence, or perhaps make the proposal irresistibly interesting or easy. The advantage of knowing your man is apparent; likewise, the techniques of persuasion and salesmanship.

9. *Working with superiors.* If your superiors are leaders, as normally they are, then it is correct to term you a follower. There is a golden rule of followership which should never be forgotten and which, if remembered, will raise fellowship to the level that it should occupy. The rule is this: Give to our superior what you would want if you were the "boss." Anticipating the future a little, we may rephrase the rule slightly: Give what you will expect when *you* are the superior.

What *will* you expect of your subordinates? You will expect a fairly long list of qualities of mind and character-qualities like loyalty, reliability, intelligence, willingness to learn, cooperativeness, initiative, perseverance, and perhaps many more. Assuming integrity of character and loyalty to the company, you will especially want men around you who will play ball and who will keep teamwork constantly in mind. When a decision is made by top management, these men will remember what teamwork demands and accept the decision without grumbling or evasion. These are the minimum traits you will want when you are in top management; they are the same traits which the present top management should find in both of you.

Followership is an art no less than leadership. It is based on right reason and hence there should be no feeling of servility in accepting its demands. It is not always easy to live up to the ideal which your own mind pictures for you, but what ideal is ever easy to live up to? The easier way is to avoid self-discipline, to relax, to evade and then excuse one's evasions. But that is not the way to business success.

10. *Check your attitude towards superiors.* It is a characteristic of our age to cultivate a cynical attitude towards business leaders, their motives and ability. The trend has an obvious source in the propaganda of those who want to undermine the American free enterprise system in favor of socialism or communism, but it has been aided by the mistakes committed by some business managements-mistakes which have drawn criticism from Americans of every economic creed, including those who believe in free enterprise.

After all faults have ben conceded, the fact remains that the sins of the few should not be imputed to the many, that top management as a group should not be held in less respect because of antisocial conduct of individuals within the group. To take any other attitude is playing the game of the propagandist or that of the bored and boring cynic.

One corrective for any tendency to become cynical is to extend one's acquaintanceship with business leaders. If this cannot be done in person, it can be done vicariously through reading. Profiles and interviews in business magazines, books of business biography are easily available at small expense. Thereby furnish the data that will revise any one-sided estimate of top management based on an unfortunate contact with the wrong kind of business leader.

11. *Dealing with the difficult superior.* In an ideal world, there would be only top executives whose personalities radiate friendliness and inspiration to their associates and assistants. Unfortunately, the world is not ideal, and executives (senior as well as junior) are not only human, but even "all too human," to borrow the famous phrase of Nietzsche. Consequently, it is easier to work with some superiors than with others. Some executives are the sort to whom it is almost instinctive to give respect and even affection. But what of the others-the executives who rasp and exasperate?

The answer must be determined with reference to the principle of teamwork. It is the team, and the team's accomplishments, that is important; the enterprise is bigger than any single individual. Except in very special circumstances, the concept of the team must prevail over any and all personal feelings. The "boss" must be presumed to be a key man in the company team, whose policies are to be upheld to win success. In no other way can teamwork be secured.

Over and above this fundamental solution to the problem, there are few other lines of action that can be taken to ease the personal burden of the difficult superior. One is to study the superior's type. Is he chronically irritable-the "old grouch type" type? Is he vain and pompous-the "show-off" type? Is he the sort who is hazy on most details but very definite on who is to blame if his hazy plans go wrong? Is he the old-fashioned "driver" who suspects everyone but himself of being constitutionally lazy or inefficient?

There are ways of handling each type, once it is determined. As a rule, the difficult superior is not a clinical case (if he were, he would hardly survive in business), and drastic measures are not required-merely the application of simple methods to bring out the man's better traits and minimize his unpleasant ones. The methods to be tries may include a little firmness, the tactful use of humor, a bit of harmless flattery, the rendering of some unexpected service, the discovery of a mutual hobby or cultural interest. The junior executive will not be discouraged if his first efforts fail to click; patient perseverance is required.

12. *The influence of high expectations*. One rule is always safe to follow, whether dealing with a difficult superior, an irritating associate, or a trying subordinate. That is the rule of acting as if you expected only the best from the other person. Make him see that you are not expecting discourtesy or childish vanity or any other unpleasant trait. By calmly refusing to accept such traits as his normal behavior, you can create a picture in the other person's mind of what he is thought to be, and in the end he is likely to try to live up to the picture he created.

If, on the other hand, we act as if we expected only the worst from the other person, our behavior suggests the unpleasant role to him. Few people are so self-centered as not to respond to the psychological force of suggestion; our manner, words and positive actions can be very influential, if they are persistent and consistent.

In the long run, of course, much depends upon ourselves. A good executive has been defined as one who knows all the people above and below him-and still likes them. It is important to probe for a man's likable traits, and to devise methods for bringing them into the foreground of the picture. Moreover, few men can long resist the solid appeal of an assistant who is growing on the job, learning how to make himself more useful, exemplifying the art of followership, contributing his share to the upbuilding of the company team. Expecting the best of others, the junior executive expects also the best of himself.

13. *Conserving the chief's time*. Efficiency is very important in preserving good relations with a senior administrator. The junior officer who wastes his chief's time through poorly prepared visits to his office is likely to find the busy signal against him. Without realizing what has happened, the younger man begins to complain that the chief is not sufficiently accessible. A few simple rules of conduct will prevent or remedy this complaint.

First and foremost, the junior executive should look far enough ahead to anticipate problems before they become urgent. Some men never sense a difficulty until it is upon them, demanding solution; consequently, they are forced to run to their chief frequently, perhaps several times a day. The man who gets into a rut like that is indulging in conduct unbecoming an executive, and can hardly blame his chief for taking down the welcome sign. Nor does he help his case by beginning each presentation of his difficulties with the monotonous question, "What shall I do?"

What he should do, of course, is to develop some overdue efficiency. Let him cultivate foresight; look ahead to see where difficulties are likely to arise; analyze them before they become urgent. The next step would be to think out some alternative solutions. Then, seeing his chief at a convenient time when there is leisure to discuss the budding problem carefully, he can submit problem and possible solutions, along with other problems, for the chief's decision.

If the junior officer has recommendations requiring his chief's approval before they can be put into effect, he should submit them to the chief in writing, especially when the proposal must be referred to a higher officer or committee. The presentation should be concise yet complete, in the form that experience has taught him will be most readable for his chief. A brief, with each point set out clearly, is usually desirable.

In this connection, it may be pointed out that the written memorandum is a great time-saver in dealing with senior executives. Some men can express themselves more concisely on paper than in conversation, and there are no interruptions to distract the writer from completing his report. In a conference, the chief's questions may cause the junior executive to lose his argument or to omit important data. From the chief's standpoint, the memorandum gives him the gist of a proposal quickly, and often he may note his decision on the margin and return the "memo" without the need for a conference.

If a conference is necessary, the junior officer should not only try to save time by being concise and factual when it is his turn to talk, but he should also be a good listener when the chief has the floor. Psychologists have discovered that people frequently think they have listened to instructions or a discussion when in reality they have let their own thoughts distract them from hearing all that the other man had to say. The ability to fix instructions clearly in mind is not as common as one might suppose; people often hear what they expect or want o hear. The remedy is to look at your chief while he is talking and concentrate on what he is saying. If he doesn't make sense, that is your cue to ask a question. Be sure you understand.

14. *Keeping the chief informed*. The administrative head of the department or division is entitled to know what is going on within his division, and will set up machinery (usually in the form of routine reports and records) to keep him informed of everything affecting the division's progress. He will depend upon his assistant's to see that system is working properly.

In addition to the information brought in by routine records and reports, the chief will expect less formal but more intimate "briefing" from his junior executives. It is especially important to acquaint him with difficulties that appear to be shaping up so that he may have time to think out any decisions that may become necessary. He wants to know about errors and delays that may affect other departments and cause friction, and the wise assistant will give the bad news along with the good. It may take a bit of courage, especially if the top executive is inclined to be excitable, but it will take even more courage if the news is held back, only to break into the open in much worse form at some later date. Bad news becomes twice as bad if it comes from some one outside the department.

The junior officer usually gets closer to the rank and file of workers than does the top management. He is therefore in a position to watch for sources of friction, dissatisfaction and defection from the ideal of teamwork. Reporting on these conditions as they begin to take shape, and submitting remedial measures for top approval, the junior executive can take an important part in maintaining good company morale.

15. *An educational opportunity*. The years spent in working with a good senior executive should be a rich and fruitful experience. In point of fact, many a business man who has passed through his apprenticeship and become a senior officer in his turn, now looks back upon his junior years as one of the happiest periods of his life.

It would be most exceptional if a junior officer did not find much to learn from his association with the division head, and with the tope officers generally. They have reached the top, in most instances, through ability and force of character; they have acquired the wisdom born of experience as they progressed upward, and have much to give. They give more as the

140

junior executive advances in his own knowledge of business principles. It takes wisdom to make use of wisdom.

18. *Working with associates*. What we said earlier in this chapter on earning cooperation, rather than commanding it, applies with particular force to the business of getting teamwork from associates-that is, from the men in other departments or from those in your own department who share your experience level.

A friendly attitude, maintenance of human respect, a recognition of the rights and interests of other executives and other departments-these are fundamental for the winning of happy and cooperative relations with associates. Friendliness should be consistent-not hot and cold. Respect should be evident, even though associates know one another well enough to indulge in considerable "kidding." Banter will stay good-natured when men respect one another and one another's contribution to the common effort.

17. *Know the other fellow's work*. Respect for other departments and their procedures should have a factual basis, will grow in proportion to a man's knowledge of what other departments contribute to the business. Some activities and routines may seem strange or even inexplicable at first contact with them, but better acquaintance will nearly always disclose their reasonableness. It is a mistake, also, to underestimate the value of any activity or service; what appears to be a very humble or even questionable service may prove to be exceedingly important in an emergency.

It has often been pointed out that international misunderstandings would be fewer and less dangerous to the world's peace if the peoples of the world were better acquainted. To that end, international associations are encouraged by peaceful governments, and other devices promoted such as the exchange of students between the universities of one country and another. The same principle applies in the smaller world of business relationships. The more we know about the tasks and problems of other departments of a business, the more easily do we avoid forming set prejudices interfering with the development of full and complete teamwork.

The means of getting acquainted with the work of associates are simple and easily cultivated. The most available is to practice being a good listener, not only giving the other fellow a chance to talk about what is uppermost on his mind but even encouraging him to talk through a tactful question or an observation on some activity of his department that has come to your attention. If you can, speak mainly of successful activities; you are more likely to get constructive information if you ask about successes. Getting a man to talk about difficulties or upsets may give *him* some relief, but your gain may be next to nil.

Now and then an opportunity will present itself for engaging in some activity requiring the physical cooperation of two departments. It may be merely lending a hand during an emergency. It may be a new routine or a company policy of more enduring character. Whatever the opportunity, it should be seized upon to deepen the mutual understanding of departmental aims and methods. To think only of the extra work involved, if such there is, is to miss an important opportunity for promoting departmental understanding and teamwork.

18. *Mistakes to avoid*. There are few errors in getting along with associates that easily recognized to be mistakes, yet, because they are mixed up so intimately with strong emotions, are committed now and then by men who know better. One such error is to carry an issue to a superior officer, over the head of an associate. Men of experience testify that this procedure can be justified only rarely, when silence would involve a major loss to the company. The right thing to do is to work patiently at the job of converting the associate to the policy that you know to be correct. To achieve permanent results, the issue should be settled directly with the man whose willing cooperation is desired.

Another error detrimental to teamwork is to feel or show jealousy over the way promotions are handed out by top management. It is emotionally disturbing, of course, when the wrong man gets promoted but the team remains more important than any individual in it. It is in this consideration that must be adhered to, no matter how your glands feel about the matter. The top officers have made their changes of rank after due deliberation and expect these changes to be accepted in good faith and given a fair trial. If their judgements are proved wrong, they will correct them.

Sometimes the junior executives, particularly if he is a newcomer to the organization, will be disturbed by finding that certain cliques exist in factory or office, or that there is a definite playing of office "politics" in an unwise endeavor to secure advancement or privilege. Either condition is unpleasant for the man who is an outsider; both will yield, in time, to a cheerful, persevering ignoring of them. Show neither resentment nor indignation, which will not get any results of the kind you want. If very bad, it would be better to seek another connection in some company where opportunities for promotion are not so rare that executives must use time and energy in establishing personal influence and preference over their associates. Usually, conditions will not be that bad, and you can safely ignore cliques and office policies so long as they do not seriously affect the success of your work. When that is endangered, it is time to lay the matter before your chief or to transfer your allegiance.

19. *Working with subordinates*. Our discussion of the cooperative process to this point should indicate pretty clearly what must be done to inspire teamwork among those under *your* supervision. Now the shoe is on the other foot; instead of being a follower, you are the leader of this segment of the company team. These workers look to you for friendly guidance, for interpretation of company policies and instructions. What you want from your chief, it is now your privilege and responsibility to give your subordinates. The mistakes of your chief-his personality faults and errors of leadership-are yours to avoid, if you can.

Teamwork is achieved through voluntary effort pooled into a common cause, with the accent on voluntary. Unless the worker's will is in it, there will be little teamwork. That will cannot be forced; that is why leadership is better than driving, and voluntary effort more effective than effort induced through fear. The driver relies upon fear-fear of ridicule, sarcasm, humiliation, or possible discharge. To a degree, he may get results, but they are short-term results. He gets other results, hidden for the moment but likely to come into the open at a later date; these are the long-term results of worker dissatisfaction, hatred and disloyalty. The ultimate, over-all result-the creation of a hard-hitting, loyal team-either is not achieved at all, or is achieved in spite of the executive's wrong-headed leadership. Workers are often a long-suffering group, forgiving much because some trait in the driver that they love or admire. Obviously, it is dangerous to count on any such miracle of followership.

The logic of the labor-management situation calls for more intelligent leadership, not less. It is, of course, far too complex a subject to cover in a few paragraphs, or even in a few chapters. Fortunately, the literature on the subject of industrial or labor relations is growing, both quantitatively and qualitatively. Not only books and brochures, but magazines and periodic services are available to the executive who wants to know more about personnel and labor management. Leadership can arm itself very easily with the principles and methods evolved from the experience of other executives and made public via the printed page. To become informed is the first step.

20. *Some first principles*. There are a few simple but effective principles whose observance will smooth the task of getting cooperation from subordinates, whether these are office, retail or factory workers. The first principle, or rule, is to be clear and definite in giving any necessary instructions. To tell workers to treat customers courteously is not enough; courtesy is a complex made up of many separate acts, phrases and attitudes, some of which will be known to any person but not all. It is the omissions from the worker's idea of courtesy that do the damage.

Too many instructions given by executives, even when put in writing, are vague as to who, what, where, when or why. For example, so simple an instruction as asking an employee to help save electricity will force if phrased in the conventional way: "Please turn out the lights." To make the instruction really specific, it should read something like this: "Each employee is requested to turn out the lights over and in front of his desk when leaving the office for lunch or at the end of the day. Unnecessary electricity bills take money needed for other purposes-payrolls, for example." Now the instruction tells who, what, where, when and why-all five of them. The extra length of the instruction will be repaid several times over if it secures wider compliance on the part of employees.

A second rule for getting teamwork is to remember the little things that make people happy on the job. A word of appreciation when work is well done, an inquiry about the worker's hobbies or family, promptness in approving reasonable requests for better or safer equipment, time out for a moment's chat about the World Series or the weather or any other small topic of the day-these are examples of how good executives keep in touch with their workers.

Remembering he little things is in reality an application of a still broader principle, that of keeping up one's interest in workers as people. The executive who thinks of his workers as co-workers-as working with the boss rather than for him-is on the inside track in labor relations. His personnel will never accuse hi, of forgetting that workers are human beings or of treating employees as mere machines-two of the commonest complaints made by workers against executives. They will feel, on the contrary, that they are associates in the business, members of the company team.